Liar Liar

Cruz on Fire

By Paul LeBon

Email: tedcruzlies@gmail.com

All Ted and Rafael Cruz Lies and Racist &
Homophobic statements are memorialized on
video

You Tube Channel
Ted Cruz & Rafael Cruz Lies
https://www.youtube.com/channel/UC_E7zWmpN-vOn-U7gAX1_Mg/feed

Dedication

I dedicate this book to my Cuban hero Jaime Cardinal Ortega y Alamino and to the many wonderful and loving Cuban men, women, and children who I have met over the time of my Mission Trips, especially one sweet angel. To the memory of Frank Pais. And lest I forget, my wing man Brady,the world's best service companion and my best Bud, Tommy Sprayberry,deaf, mute, and intellectually challenged but the kindest person you'll ever meet..

"El Bueno no tener pelos en la lengua"
"LeBon does not have hair on his tongue"- Cuban expression

Acknowledgements

I want to acknowledge the help and contributions of the following: Professor Louise Doire of the College of Charleston, Mindy Hollings, Bill and Shelli Neal, Alfonso, Ernesto, Luis Enrique, Elgis, Jose, Yohandra, Yaneli, Mario, Beatriz, and Luis, fine Cuban Nationals all, as well as several Cuban functionaries.

To Ole and staff at McDonald's on FM407 in Lewisville for their delicious coffee and quiet workspace. And to the gang at Razzoo's in Lewisville for helping to recharge my batteries every Sunday after Mass: Avery, Bri, Courtney, Jordan, Kennedy, Lauren, Noelanie, Olivia, Raquel, and David - the host with the most.

Lie; verb: *to make an untrue statement with intent to deceive; to create a false or misleading impression*
- Merriam Webster

"A lie is something you make up and say with the intent to deceive."

Mark Davis, Dallas/Fort Worth Talk Show Host & Unabashed Cruz supporter

"If you tell the lie often enough, people believe it."

Mike Gallagher, Syndicated Talk Host
'The Happy Conservative Warrior', World Class Exaggerator

"If you always tell the truth, the details will never change."

Narcisse LeBon 1917 – 1997 6th grade dropout during the Great Depression

"Me, I always tell the truth.
Even when I lie."
Tony Montana, most famous Cuban-American
dishwasher of the 20th Century
(Al Pacino in Scarface)

"Lies upon lies upon lies upon lies."
Rafael Cruz, most famous Cuban-American
Dishwasher of the 21st Century

Guess who was a legal immigrant,
and possessed a work visa?

Rafael Bienvenido Cruz Diaz
&
Rafael Edward 'Ted' Cruz

Biggest Cuban-American Con Artists

since

Rosie Ruiz Vivas
Boston Marathon Cheater, 1980

Table of Contents

Rafael Bienvenido Cruz Diaz Birth Certificate
Cuba, not Kenya, nor Indonesia
(enhanced wording for legibility)

Introduction

It was early 2012 when I first heard parts of the story. I was preparing to head to Cuba where I was engaged in Catholic Mission activities and preparing for the visit by Pope Benedict XVI. A political ad came on TV for Ted Cruz[1], candidate for US Senate and someone I knew very little about. The ad started with the words, "He comes from a family of fighters . . ." Then a figure of a man appeared on the screen.

The man wore thick-framed eyeglasses, had a beard, and appeared to be in his 20's or older. Then photos flashed on the screen of Cuban Dictator Fulgencio Batista who was eventually overthrown by Fidel Castro, and photos of Castro himself. The ad concludes with Ted Cruz and his father walking in a park. I made a mental note to look up Rafael Cruz after the elections because I felt it would be nice to have someone talk Cuba with who knew the country.

I didn't pay much attention to father or son because of my commitments in Cuba until later in the year after Ted Cruz had won Texas' US Senate seat. I was sitting in a doctor's waiting room thumbing through

---

[1] https://www.youtube.com/watch?v=O0ePwy6Q0UM

a local 'mailbox' newspaper called *the Cross Timbers Gazette*. I came across a story titled *Only in America*[2] which was about Rafael Cruz..

The article gushed with profuse praise for the man but was filled with statements that I knew from my experience in Cuba were just not true. (*"Mr. Cruz knows better than most about the horrible conditions under which people are forced to live in a Socialist [read: communist] dictatorship. He grew up in Cuba under the tyrannical rule of Fulgencio Batista. When he was 17, he was arrested and charged with speaking out against the government. During his incarceration, he was severely beaten by prison guards every four hours"*) I wasn't sure who was exaggerating the facts; Rafael Cruz or the writer who has a knack for embellishment. (Rafael claims he was 18, but accuracy is not one of that writer's strong points)

I've conducted 12 mission trips to Cuba, have visited 96 parishes, and possess a very good sense of the real history of Cuba over the past 60 years. I decided to look deep into Rafael Cruz's claim of his 'amazing life story'.

---

[2] http:// http://www.crosstimbersgazette.com/opinion/2733-only-in-america?format=pdf

You Tube has a plethora of videos containing speeches delivered by Rafael Cruz that I began watching I could barely believe what I was hearing - simple facts twisted so out of proportion and distorted. Racism, Homophobic rants; I was somewhat disgusted and sickened.

I decided to conduct an experiment. In videotaped speeches, Cruz told audiences that his mother – a public school teacher - did not want to teach Marxism as ordered by Castro '*so she faked an attack of insanity*; *running up and down the halls screaming, pulling her hair out, and foaming at the mouth.*' Tea Party audiences in the videos bought this story hook, line, and sinker.

I wrote about this alleged insanity attack on my Blog, *Cuba 54*. I created a false Facebook member and asked to be friended by Rafael B. Cruz. Once my friend request was accepted I posted on his FB page for all his Facebook friends to see that there is no such thing as 'an attack of insanity' and I believed Rafael Cruz had made that wild story up. I made reference to my blog in the Facebook post. The Facebook comments section filled up with Tea Partiers defending the man and attacking my pseudonym. Within two hours my post was removed and I was de-friended by Rafael B. Cruz. All his 'evangelical' followers then came after me in the comments section of my Blog which, fortunately I had to approve before they could appear online. These people had the same rabid tenacity and belief in their 'messiah' as the Jim Jones and David Koresh followers had had. These self -labeled christians (lower case 'c' intentional) made the most vile and offensive comments. How dare I attack the saintly man who survived torture and was chosen by God to be the father of America's savior?

I received a surprise later on when I saw a video of Rafael Cruz addressing a group of conservative Republicans at a Freedom Works event in Salt Lake City in July 2013. He fed the crowd his usual shtick of lies and fabrications, but something changed when he got to his post-Revolution lies. When he got to the lie about Castro ordering teachers to teach Marxism, he said that his mother refused and *SHE WAS FIRED*. I was on to something. This left me wondering, if Rafael Cruz changes his story so quickly could a book that points out and debunks Rafael Cruz's many lies cause him to finally come clean about his 'heroic tale' of fighting in the Cuban Revolution? Might he eventually fess up that his story of guerilla warfare, arrest, and torture, and immigration to the United States is a full blown fabrication?

I've come to view Rafael Cruz as a One Act, One Actor Play. He is quite a showman. He never falters, he tells the same stories, and he uses the same words, same emphasis, and always the same body language. He is a very well-rehearsed stage actor: part actor; part showman; part carnival barker.

How would a full expose of 'the pretend pastor' Rafael Bienvenido Cruz Diaz's stories sit with the 8 – 10 audiences of Tea Party and pastors' conferences that he appears before every month? Here is just a synopsis of the 'whoppers', though there are many more – 76 in all - contained and disproved in this book:

- at the age of 14 he became involved in a Revolution, and for four years was engaged in sabotage, propaganda, training, and collecting weapons
- he was arrested, put in a 7' x 7' cell with a 1000 watt light bulb at a military garrison in his hometown of Matanzas, and beaten and tortured every four hours by soldiers, only to be released by a colonel after a moonlight tour of the city

- a lady from the underground came to see him after his release and told him the Revolution said he had to leave the country for his safety at age 18

- he applied to three universities in the US by submitting letters without any transcripts in June or July 1957, was accepted by the University of Texas within a few weeks, and headed to Austin in August, 1957 to start classes in September

- made it to Austin, Texas a month before school started, penniless and only with the clothes on his back; was given a Social Security card at the INS offices, got a job as a dishwasher earning 50 cents per hour, worked full-time, went to school full time, paid his way through UT

- stuffed himself with food during his eight hour work shift so he did not have to buy meals the other 16 hours

- went to the movies and watched them play over again and taught himself to speak English in only 30 days

Rafael Cruz is a political Bernie Madoff. He has created an overarching sham that people buy hook, line, and sinker. Madoff robbed people of their financial resources; Rafael Cruz has robbed them of their trust and common sense. I am sure many people upon reading this book will feel violated. Yet other sycophants who put blind loyalty ahead of truth and common sense will fall in step and continue to drink Cruz's Kool Aid and attack me and those who refute Rafael Cruz's lies.

Compiling seventy six major deceptions from a person's oral autobiography, many repeated as gospel by his son - a presidential candidate – is quite overwhelming. My father lied to my siblings and me: get to bed or Santa won't come; I saw the tooth fairy slip into your room; be careful camping in the woods, Fingernail Freddie is out there.

But for a man and his son to collaborate and fabricate an entire life story to help fuel the son's presidential ambition is both narcissistic and amoral.

See the Introduction of 'Pastor' Cruz
At the California Eagle Forum
On You Tube[3]

Keep your tongue from evil And your lips from speaking deceit.
– Psalms 34: 12-13

Therefore, laying aside falsehood, speak truth each one of you
with his neighbor for we are members of one another. -
Ephesians 4:25

Do not lie to one another, since you laid aside the old self with
its evil practices. – Colossians 3:9-10

You shall not steal, nor deal falsely, nor lie to one another.
'You shall not swear falsely by My name, so as to profane the
name of your God; I am the LORD. – Leviticus 19:11-12

Lying lips are an abomination to the LORD, -Proverbs 12:22

The heart is more deceitful than all else – Jeremiah 17:9

Above dedicated to Pastor Rafael Cruz and Senator Ted Cruz

---

[3] https://www.youtube.com/watch?v=lkjguo5WZl4

Chapter 1

Lie # 1

"I grew up in Cuba under a strong, military, oppressive dictatorship." [4]

Cuba has been involved in revolutions on and off since 1868. Rafael Cruz was born in 1939. Fulgencio Batista was the democratically elected president in 1940 in conjunction with a new Constitution. He left office per the Constitution in 1944. Ramon Grau San Martin was elected in a free election in 1944 and left under the Constitution in 1948. Carlos Prío Socarrás was elected president, again in a free election in 1948.[5]

Fulgencio Batista filed as a candidate to regain the presidency in an election scheduled for June, 1952. Fearful that he would lose, he jumped the gun and staged a coup on March 10, 1952.[6] Most dictatorships are usually military dictatorships, all top government positions are held by military officers.

This was not the case in Batista's Cuba; senior government ministers were civilians, most notably

---

[4] https://www.youtube.com/watch?v=8S7e5eSRcdU
[5] HistoryofCuba.com
[6] Ibid

Interior Minister Rafael Diaz Balart. Fulgencio Batista almost never appeared in public in military garb.

Most importantly, freedom of speech, assembly, or the press was not immediately constricted. Batista's interest was not in controlling the lives of his people. He had two goals: 1.) to be accepted by the middle class who had rejected his attempts to join their social clubs during his first term because he was a mulatto; and 2.) having his hands out to be filled with cash by the US Mafia – the island's casino and brothel operators. Rafael Cruz grew up in a free and open country which started subtle changes when he was 13 years old.

In time, the Batista Dictatorship would become oppressive, but it was never military in nature as were Hussein in Iraq, Amin in Uganda, Kaddafi in Libya, Pinochet in Chile, Pol Pot in Cambodia, or Noriega in Panama.

The only portion of Rafael Cruz's statement above that is accurate? The first five words - 'I grew up in Cuba'.

Cuban Commentary: *Batista had no interest in being 'El Jefe'. He wanted his hands in the pockets of the America*

Mafia.[7] - Alfonso, age 83 (Translated and edited for clarity)

[7] http://www.pbs.org/wgbh/amex/castro/peopleevents/p_batista.html
'Status Seeker'

Chapter 2

Lie # 2

"So I found myself at age14 involved in a Revolution [8]

    It seems ludicrous to think that Rafael Cruz would have joined a revolution before he even entered the 9th grade against the hand that was feeding his parents. But more importantly there was not a revolution going on in his 14th year. It did not commence full bore until his 18th year, seven months before he would leave for the University of Texas.

    January 17, 1957 is when the war actually began. It was a raid by rebels on a small army garrison at the mouth of the Plata River. [9]

Cuban Commentary: *The Revolution was started in 1957 by Movimiento 26 de Julio; M-26-7. When he was 14 this boy was still picking his nose. – Ernesto, deceased 2014 at age 86 (Translated and edited for clarity)*

---

[8] https://www.youtube.com/watch?v=tMBuLyp1tMl
[9] HistoryofCuba.com

Chapter 3

Lie # 3

"And of course as it happened with every revolution, where do you think it started? It started in the high schools and universities." [10]

Cuba had been in a frequent state of revolution since 1868 when Carlos Manuel de Céspedes freed his slaves to help fight for independence from Spain. In 1879 Calixto Garcia attempted to start a revolution but failed. In 1892 an exiled dissident living in New York named Jose Marti organized the Cuban Revolutionary Party seeking to gain independence from Spain. These are the most well-known and respected Cuban revolutionary leaders.

Though there were several more attempted uprisings in the 20th century, every revolution lacked one element which Rafael Cruz mentions in all of his speeches - that all revolutions were started in the high schools and universities. This Revolution was started by Fidel Castro and his brother Raul and other rebels. There eventually were three groups of University students that

---

[10] https://www.youtube.com/watch?v=GqQnwPsK9To

became involved, the FEU in Santiago de Cuba[11] and the DRE[12] and AAA,[13] both in Havana. But high school students – who still lived at home – could not participate to any degree and usually only were involved if they had an older brother involved who could vouch for them, especially if they lived in outlier cities such as Matanzas like Rafael Cruz.

Cuban Commentary: *This boy started the Revolution? Fidel must be very grateful. Luis Enrique, age 26 (Translated and edited for clarity)*

---

[11] La Federación Estudiantil Universitaria
[12] Directorio Revolucionario Estudiantil
[13] AAA Estudiantil Habana

Chapter 4

Lie #4

"So, I spent nearly four years involved in sabotage, and propaganda, and trying to collect weapons and training and so on and so forth."[14]

Following his timeline, we are supposed to believe that Rafael Cruz 'became involved in the revolution' at age 14 (1953) and spent the next four years as a revolutionary involved in. sabotage, propaganda, and collecting weapons. (Thru 1957) There are two major factors that undercut Lies # 4 and #5.

In 1953, the Revolution was initiated with a one day event, the Raid on the Moncada Barracks (military facility) by Fidel Castro and his followers; supported by female medics. (160 total persons) They battled Batista's military troops.[15] There were no high school or university students involved.

The day was July 26 – a date which lives in Cuban lore. The skirmish lasted one day – many of Castro's rebels were killed, he and Raul and the other survivors hid out in the jungle. They were captured by the military five days later in huts in the jungle and were put

---

[14] https://www.youtube.com/watch?v=8K0c7vV_cBA
[15] Quartered at Moncada Barracks in Santiago de Cuba

on trial. Fidel Castro was kept in solitary confinement awaiting trial.

They would all be tried – men and women (nurses) and sentenced to prison. Fidel was tried last. He represented himself and his closing argument which ended with the words *'History Will Absolve Me'* was eventually printed and distributed to Cuba's peasants.[16] Castro was sentenced to 15 years. Eventually public opinion ran in his favor and people clamored for his release so Batista released him and his rebels and nurses from prison on May 15, 1955.[17]

Castro and his men left Cuba on June 24, 1955 and went into exile in Mexico.[18] They would return on December 2, 1956 aboard a yacht called the Granma bound for Santiago. They were three days late due to weather; they had been expected on November 30. On November 30 there was a battle between the military and Castro's supporters as well as 300 members of the FEU (Federacion de Etudiantes Universidad – Federation of University Students) in support of the rebels' arrival.[19]

---

[16] HistoryofCuba.com
[17] Ibid
[18] Ibid
[19] Ibid

The students were under the leadership of a 22
year old named Frank Pais.[20] This was a four day
uprising, and it is important to point out that 300
university students were from the University of the
Oriente and other colleges and were local to the Santiago
area. There was no high school student involvement in
any way. The students were all dressed in uniforms that
the women of Santiago had secretly sewn for them late at
night in their homes. They wore green and red armbands.

Many of Castro's rebels and university students
were killed. Those that were not killed were rounded up
and shot in the head by the Cuban National Police.[21]

In lies to be exposed later in this book, Rafael
Cruz attempts to co-op Frank Pais' bravery and valor.
Rafael Cruz also claims that when students were being
shot in the head left and right that God saved him from
the killing because God had bigger plans for Rafael's
life.[22]

There would be no outward revolutionary
activities until the first battle of the war, January 17, 1957
– seven months before Rafael Cruz departed for the
University of Texas at Austin. There were however no

[20] Frank Pais – Chapter 89
[21] Rafael Cruz Lie # 35 - https://www.youtube.com/watch?v=ktyx_7-JRcc
[22] Rafael Cruz Lie # 39 - https://www.youtube.com/watch?v=oA_lAJEAxKs

skirmishes between university students (FEU, DE, and AAA) and Batista's police. There were no battles; the student group would pull a raid on a location and get away, hopefully before the police arrived. Only two prominent events involving university students occurred, the attack on the Presidential Palace and the Cuban National Radio station which took place on March 13, 1957 and will be discussed in detail in Chapter 12. One can track the History of Cuba from 1929 to December 31, 1958 and see there were no battles, no fights between high school students and Batista's soldiers, nor any other conflict which Rafael Cruz and Ted Cruz fabricated to dupe gullible audiences.[23]

On January 17, 1957 the war opened with a successful rebel attack on a small Army Garrison at the Mouth of the La Plata River. The rebel Army had a mere 23 weapons.[24]

Had Rafael Cruz really spent four years engaged in the activities he takes credit for, they would have likely taken place in Santiago, home of the Moncada Barracks, sentimental cradle of the Revolution, site of Castro's eventual return from exile in Mexico, and the hub of unrest and activity during Castro's absence. How would a

---

[23] http://www.historyofcuba.com/history/time/timetbl3.htm
[24] Ibid

14 year old boy 830 km from home have fed himself, where would he have lived, and how would he have attended school? There is no doubt that if challenged with this question Rafael Cruz would concoct a response like 'a family took me in and the mother home-schooled me'. (A plug for one of the Tea Party's favorite anti-Socialist strategies – home school) That might be difficult considering in another speech he stated that he 'got all A's in high school' but he would likely just chalk it off to the Grace of God.

Cuban Commentary: *He claims to have done these things in Matanzas? He must take people for fools to believe him. - Matanzas resident Elgis, age 62(Translated and edited for clarity)*

Chapter 5

Lie # 5

"At that time, a young charismatic leader rose up talking about 'Hope and Change'. His name was Fidel Castro. We thought he was going to be our liberator so we all followed him blindly." [25]

If you follow Rafael Cruz's tale here, Rafael Cruz and his high school friends along with some university associates started the Revolution and Fidel Castro – a young charismatic leader - came along and joined the effort. Cubans who knew him personally tell me that Fidel wasn't especially charismatic at that time - charismatic people are out and about meeting and greeting people and that was not Fidel.

This lie is designed to bolster Rafael Cruz's assertion that President Barack Obama is a Marxist just like Fidel because Hope and Change was President Obama's campaign slogan in 2008 and Obama was young and charismatic.

The truth is, not only did Fidel not talk about 'Hope and Change' but Fidel was not traveling the countryside speaking out about anything. Fidel had graduated from a Jesuit High School in 1944, and was

---

[25] https://www.youtube.com/watch?v=e2JuwuAji7U

rated as the best baseball player in the country. Rather than play baseball professionally he chose the university of Havana and Law School.[26] In 1948 he traveled to Bogota, Columbia to participate in a Revolution.[27] In 1950, he graduated from law school and ran for Congress, losing the election.[28]

In 1952 Fulgencio Batista filed to run for President but fearing he might lose the June election he staged a bloodless coup d'état on March 10.

Batista allowed his American gangster friend Meyer Lansky who controlled the casinos and brothels to establish Cuba as an international drug trafficking port.[29] It was then that Fidel Castro began planning for the revolution and the raid on the Moncada Barracks. During the Revolution from February, 1958 until January 1, 1959, Fidel Castro was heard in interviews on Radio Rebelde from his stronghold in La Plata. He delivered one on-air speech on August 18, 1958. He never mentioned Hope and Change. [30]

The most egregious part of this lie is that Rafael Cruz seeks to steal Fidel Castro's valor as the instigator

---

[26] HistoryofCuba.com
[27] Ibid
[28] Ibid
[29] http://www.u-s-history.com/pages/h1768.html
[30] https://en.wikipedia.org/wiki/Radio_Rebelde

and mastermind of the Cuban Revolution, claiming credit for him and other high school students. The raid on the Moncada Barracks led by Fidel Castro took place before Rafael Cruz even entered 9th grade, on July 26, 1953.

Eventually, the name of Castro's revolutionary movement would come to be called the *26th of July Movement.* But the fact that audiences always react so overtly to this lie shows just how gullible Tea Party members and Evangelicals are. Even Rush Limbaugh praised Rafael Cruz for telling this lie and 'hitting it out of the park.' So this shows that there is not only honor among thieves but also honor among liars.

Cuban Commentary: *I lived in Santa Clara. We knew very little about Fidel before the Moncada raid. He did not travel making orations. Of course after Moncada he was in prison then went to Mexico. –Jose, age 68 (Translated and edited for clarity)*

Chapter 6

Lie #6

"1957 I made the mistake of trying to recruit somebody who was a government informant and I was arrested."[31]

This is highly doubtful; considering this is the time he would have been preparing to graduate from high school in Matanzas, and go on to University in the US, likely having never participated in any revolutionary activities. He told *National Review Online* that he returned home from battle and was arrested sometime in either June or July, 1957.[32] He didn't remember which month? He wants people to believe he spent four years in Santiago 830 km – 515 miles away from home - as a revolutionary.

If he did spend that time in Santiago how did he attend school grades 9 - 12? School officials in Santiago would not have allowed a 14 year old boy unaccompanied by parents to have enrolled in school. Especially not one who was so busy fighting a non-existent revolution. He might have been a disruptive force in the student body.

---

[31] https://www.youtube.com/watch?v=rgiwVIQ46EM
[32] Exile and the Revolution, 11-4-11 Mario Loyola

Is it rather bizarre that he does not remember in which month he was arrested and tortured?

Cuban Commentary: *He had been in Santiago four years and then he returned to Matanzas? Where did he attend school? - Yohandra, 33 (Translated and edited for clarity)*

Chapter 7

Lie # 7

"I was in an army garrison; not technically in prison but in a cell in an army garrison."[33]

Let us start with the basics – there was no military garrison in Rafael Cruz's hometown of Matanzas in 1957. Case closed.

Cuban Commentary: *He thought he would be able to fool people into believing there was a military garrison in Matanzas. I bet he could get La Cochino Ileana Ros to swear it is true. - Elgis, age 62 (Translated and edited for clarity)*
Sarah denied it however, saying, "I did not laugh"; for she was afraid. And the Lord said, "No, but you did laugh – Genesis 18:15

---

[33] https://www.youtube.com/watch?v=L9lz-SarSgw

Chapter 8

Lie #8

"In a little cell about 7' x 7' with nothing but a concrete floor and about a thousand watt reflector on top."[34]

It has already been proved that there was no military garrison in Matanzas. It's also a fact that no one was kept in custody more than a few hours before they were killed. Quite frankly it's surprising that Rafael Cruz didn't exaggerate the size of the cell as smaller. A thousand watt reflector; this would have caused burns to the skin, would it not? Does he have any scars?

Cuban Commentary: *There was no imaginary garrison in Matanzas in 1957. - Elgis, age 62 (Translated and edited for clarity)*

---

[34] https://www.youtube.com/watch?v=ki00SO3wiV0

Chapter 9

Lie #9

"Severely tortured, beaten half to death. And they would beat me to a pulp to where nothing hurt. You were totally numb. They would throw you in that prison cell for about four hours. Now let me tell you four hours later even your hair hurt. And then they would take you out and do it again. And this went on around the clock for several days"[35]

Soldiers did not take prisoners nor torture them. Prisoners were handled by the Cuban police, part of the Cuban Interior Ministry under the direction of Rafael Diaz Balart.[36] The police did not torture prisoners as a rule – they simply killed them by putting a bullet in their head. The two prominent exceptions were 14 year old William Soler[37] and Frank Pais[38], leader of the FEU who led the support for Fidel Castro when he and his men returned from Mexican exile. Pais had escaped Santiago and was able to hideout until July 31, 1957. When the

---

[35] https://www.youtube.com/watch?v=hzHm06naVnl
[36] Rafael Diaz Balart Chapter 91
[37] William Soler – Chapter 88
[38] Frank Pais – Chapter 89

police located him he was dragged out into the street, tortured and then shot in the head. On the few known occasions when the police tortured a prisoner, it was not on again off again until your hair hurt. No, those who were tortured by the Cuban police in very sadistic ways were tortured non-stop until they succumbed or received a bullet in the head.[39] Even the gruesome Humboldt Street Massacre in Havana was pulled off by police Colonel Esteban Ventura Novo and his men, not the military.[40]

The odd aspect of this lie is that for such a prodigious liar, Rafael Cruz gave no description or embellishments of his torture. I have heard several Vietnam-era POWs speak through the years.[41] They all discussed some of the techniques used on them, as well as the goal of the torture. Rafael Cruz never says they were torturing him to learn 'X'. Another point along these lines, most torture victims have scars: on their face, neck, or other body parts that they show or talk about. Not a word from Rafael Cruz, and his face and hands are blemish free. The only part of his body Rafael Cruz

---

[39] http://www.pbs.org/wgbh/amex/castro/peopleevents/p_batista.html 'Instability'
[40] http://cuba1952-1959.blogspot.com/2009/07/1957-humboldt-7-massacre.html
[41] John McCain, Jeremiah Denton, Sam Johnson

mentions is that at the end of the torture sessions his hair hurt. How bizarre. However historic facts undermine Rafael Cruz's self-serving lies.

After the November 30, 1956 uprising, *the police were given the power to enter homes and to arrest at will*[42]. Not the Army. They were busy trying to figure out how to stop tripping over themselves and defeat Castro and his 300 or so guerillas. After all, they only had 37,000 troops. Some became notorious for their treatment of prisoners, tearing the names of sympathizers out of them in police-station basements.

They entered restaurants, eating without paying, killing rivals in love and business, raping women with no fear of investigation or prosecution. The movement organized to strike back, assassinating some of the worst torturers, taking reprisals against the police whenever a revolutionary was killed. These retaliatory measures made the M-26-7 even more popular. I have met individuals who participated in the assassination of some of Rafael Diaz Balart's dirty cops. They pride themselves on never having tortured one dirty cop, and of always depositing the body where it could be found and turned

---

[42] https://en.wikipedia.org/wiki/Cuban_Revolution

over to the man's survivors. That was a far more dignified execution that Fulgencio Batista and his chief assassin Rafael Diaz Balart, his favorite killers the Masferrer Brothers, and his battalions of dirty cops inflicted on innocent civilians.

Cuban Commentary: *Soldiers did not take prisoners. The police shot them in the head with a gun and killed them. Then they would go to their house and rape the wife and steal any possessions they wanted. – Alfonso, age 83 (Translated and edited for clarity)*

Chapter 10

Lie # 10

"I remember the last day, I got taken out of my cell about 2:00 in the morning put in a jeep with four other soldier and they said to me "Look they are going to kill you in the morning, we just wanted you to see the city for the last time."[43]

Matanzas is nothing to look at now at night and was probably less so in 1957. I doubt that the sole prisoner ever allegedly held by soldiers would have been given such first class tourist treatment. Matanzas happened to be Raphael Cruz's hometown; why didn't Raphael Cruz plead with the soldiers to drive him by his family home to say one last goodbye to his parents and sister?

Cuban Commentary: *A tour of the city before being killed? Maybe that's the treatment they gave to privileged children? Why didn't they take him to a prostitute with a bottle of rum and really send him off smiling. Yaneli, age 46 (Translated and edited for clarity)*

---

[43] https://www.youtube.com/watch?v=wuH-qCnYlXs

Chapter 11

Lie # 11

*"One with a pistol in his hand and there was another
with a hand grenade and his finger on the ring."*[44]

Let's begin with the basic premise that Cuban
military jeeps were rather small, smaller than US
versions. If you ever travel to Cuba visit the Museum of
the Revolution in either Havana or Santiago and they
have some on display. Rafael would likely have been
stuffed between the two occupants of the back of the jeep
and would have been hard-pressed to wring himself out
of there and get away.

Let's hope the soldier supposedly with his pistol
ready had the safety set, because in these narrow and
bumpy conditions bad things can happen.

As for the soldier with a hand grenade and his
finger on the pin, a more asinine story could not have
been concocted by actor Jim Carey in *'Liar Liar'*. The
streets in Matanzas were not then nor are they now
smooth boulevards. They were rough and cratered; some
were not even paved. Rafael Cruz expects people to
believe that this really happened because it buffs up his

---

[44] https://www.youtube.com/watch?v=5Z5oKHRPX7U

street cred and makes him look like some Jason Bourne character.

No military soldier would *ever* engage in such risky behavior with the lives of three colleagues and a prisoner at stake. One road bump or some jostling could have spelled death if the pin came out of the grenade.

Likewise the soldier would not have risked the chance that the burly Rafael Cruz (photo page 185) could have tried to grab the grenade from him, killing everyone in the jeep.

Cuban Commentary: *Are there never experienced military people in his audiences to say, 'wait that would have been dangerous'. Pablo, age 64 (Translated and edited for clarity)*

Chapter 12

Lie # 12

"That morning the Colonel decided to turn me loose.
They brought me to his office and he said, 'we're gonna
release you; but if a bomb explodes anywhere in the city,
we're going to pick you up.' And I said to that colonel,
'How can I be responsible what other people do?' He
looked me in the eye (cue the dramatic music) he said, 'I
don't care, if a bomb explodes in this city we're coming
to get you.'[45]

After a moonlight tour of the city, it's surprising that the Colonel didn't lay out brunch for Rafael Cruz with a nice vase of flowers as a centerpiece.

This story is a way for Rafael Cruz to tee up the mother of all lies, that God saved his life because he had special plans for him, 'father of the anointed one'. One bomb did go off while Rafael Cruz was packing his bags to move to the United States and the University of Texas. The Tinguaro Mill in Matanzas was bombed on May 27, 1957.[46]

---

[45] https://www.youtube.com/watch?v=QBg7gbsxEvk
[46] HistoryofCuba.com

This would have been before he claims he was arrested. Why wasn't his torture focused on what knowledge he might have had of who had blown up the mill? Why didn't he get a bullet in the head on the Colonel's orders just to have a scapegoat for the bombing and to strike fear in the community? After all, under Interior Minister Rafael Diaz Balart, every Cuban activist was guilty without the chance of being proven innocent.

According to the *National Review Online* article written by Cuban-American sycophant Mario Loyola, our hero had made his way back from Santiago de Cuba to Matanzas after the ill-fated return of Castro aboard the Granma in December, 1956 a distance of 830 kilometers traveling eastbound. Loyola also states in his story that Rafael Cruz was arrested, tortured and then released in June or July, 1957.

The two notable student led events after Castro's return occurred on March 13, 1957 when Rafael Cruz claims he was back in Matanzas, a mere 86 kilometers from Havana. University of Havana student leader José Antonio Echeverría led a group of students to the National Radio Station of Cuba at the time when most Cubans listened to a popular radio program. Their goal was to take over the radio station and broadcast an anti-Batista speech to the country.

Echeverria figured they could only hold the station for three minutes so he wrote and delivered a speech that he finished at the 181st second. He and his compatriots escaped the station but were pursued by Cuban police. He was shot and killed on the sidewalk on the north side of the campus. Today a plaque marks the spot.

Earlier that day a group of students had stormed the Presidential Palace with the intention of assassinating Fulgencio Batista. Most were killed by the Cuban police; four of the leaders managed to escape to their student apartment. They hid out until April 20, 1957 at which time the Cuban Police under the direction of Interior Minister Rafael Diaz Balart stormed the apartment and killed the four in cold blood in what would come to be known as the Humbolt Street Massacre. The scene was so bloody Batista ordered pictures run on the front pages of all the newspapers in the country to scare off potential revolutionaries.

I mention these events to illustrate how courageous student revolutionaries acted against a corrupt regime that had become bloody thirsty – a regime that is still revered by the morally bankrupt Cuban-American members of the United States Congress and Senate who support and protect murderous terrorists and who still drive the US Embargo against Cuba. These chapters are after all about a pathological liar – Rafael Bienvenido Cruz Diaz - who claims to have been a leader of that movement.

This begs the question – where was Rafael Cruz on March 13, 1957? Purchasing luggage for his long-planned trip to Austin, Texas? Why wasn't he in Havana taking part in either of these two historic events? He might have even ended up with his name on the honor rolls in the Museums of the Revolution where he is conspicuously unnamed.

And one final thought; it is very apparent how cold and bloody the Batista Regime had become by the Spring of 1957. Is it possible to believe that they would have wasted time torturing Rafael Cruz for several days, and then set him free? No; they would have put a bullet in his head the moment they took him into custody.

Cuban Commentary: *Personal visit with the Colonel and set free? This boy really was privileged. Of course the Colonel would have wanted to impress Diaz Balart that he had caught the Tinguaro Mill bomber so he probably would have tortured and killed him. No matter if he was not the bomber the Colonel would have had a dead body for a trophy. – Ernesto, deceased 2014 age 86 (Translated and edited for clarity)*

Chapter 13

Lie # 13

"My father took me home I was 18 years old." [47]

The father was a salesman for RCA and the mother was a public school teacher. The Batista Regime would have punished the parents for the actions of their son.

He told *National Review Online* this occurred in either June or July of 1957[48]. He cannot remember the dates he was supposedly imprisoned, tortured, taken on a moonlight ride, and then released?

How is it that his father took him home? Did the 'soldiers' or the 'colonel' call his parents and say, "We have your son here, we've been torturing him. We were going to kill him and gave him a moonlight tour of the city but we decided to let him go. Can you please come pick him up? He's bleeding all over the nice carpet."

In a lie that Ted Cruz tells in a Commencement speech at Hillsdale University in 2013, Ted claims Rafael

---

[47] https://www.youtube.com/watch?v=XMnRmKwRCyk
[48] Exile and the Revolution, 11-4-11 Mario Loyola

Cruz's teeth were kicked out during the torture.[49] Why did his father take him home? Why didn't he take him to a hospital since he had been beaten and tortured so badly, or at least to a dentist?

Cuban Commentary: *If his entire story was true, his father would have joined him in prison, and they would have both gotten bullets in the head. Then his mother and sister would have been raped, and their home robbed by the Cuban police. – Alfonso, age 83 (Translated and edited for clarity)*

---

[49] Ted Cruz Lie – Chapter 47 - https://www.youtube.com/watch?v=3U-uOTJaSq0

Chapter 14

Lie #14

"I had been home for about an hour and a lady from the Underground who I didn't know came and said 'look you're being followed there are two people assigned to follow you around the clock in shifts of eight hours'. She brought me to window of the living room and said 'you see that guy on that corner, and that guy on that other corner, those are the two assigned to follow you now."[50]

There was no underground by name. The entire movement was underground in both Havana and Santiago. The Underground is generally an entity that supports a military operation. If she had existed, the woman would have been from *The Movement* which is how Castro's rebel forces identified themselves. She arrived at his house barely one hour after Rafael Cruz and his father - pretty quick action considering they did not have texting back then. Rafael Cruz told *D Magazine*[51] that he enjoys old TV programs including *Hogan's Heroes*.

---

[50] https://www.youtube.com/watch?v=fxFFMX3ndQ4
[51] D Magazine, January 2014

Who were the most frequent walk-ons on *Hogan's Heroes*? Women from the Underground, usually pretty German or French lasses, amply proportioned to distract the Nazis and to give Colonel Hogan a little squeeze.

Back to the point of the two men following him 24 x 7: since they were both standing on corners at the front of his house, were they Barney Fife stand-ins? Why not just slip out the back door and get away?

It is difficult to believe that the Batista Regime would have expended the resources to follow a teenager, when the preferred method of dealing with troublemakers was a bullet to the head.

Cuban Commentary: *This boy had a very wild imagination to think that two men would have followed him around the clock. They tortured and killed Frank Pais in one afternoon. Pais would have been of value to follow. But not this (expletive deleted). He would not have been worth following. - Raul, age 43(Translated and edited for clarity)*

Chapter 15

Lie # 15a

So I said, "Well, I want to go to the mountains. And she said 'I'm sorry it's impossible, Batista had at that time a very substantial raid and the mountains are surrounded.' And she says 'The Revolution says the best thing you can do is leave the country."[52]

Two US reporters got into the Sierra Maestra during this period in 1957 to interview Castro. New York Times reporter Herb Matthews visited on February 17 and Robert Taber CBS newsman visited on April 23. Both got into the mountains without any problems.

Batista didn't push toward the mountains until May 24, 1958 with an undertaking known as Operation Verano. [53] Batista sent 12,000 of his 37,000 troops to coke supply lines to the rebels. Though the rebels only numbered 300 they pushed the troops back on their heels. This was when Rafael Cruz was finishing his first year of studies at the University of Texas and supposedly working as a dishwasher. The Sierra Maestra Mountains were in fact 830 km from Rafael's home. He wanted to

---

[52] https://youtu.be/h1daylyahdQ

[53] https://en.wikipedia.org/wiki/Operation_Verano

go to the mountains but how would he have gotten there, especially since he was under 24/7 government surveillance?

There was no such thing as 'The Revolution'. Castro's organization was known as the *26th of July Movement*, or simply *'The Movement'* memorializing the date of the raid on the Moncada Barracks in 1953.

The 26th of July Movement never had more than 300 men, and the numbers were fluid. With such low headcount vis-à-vis Batista's military and police why the 26th of July Movement would have directed a strong, healthy 18 year old to leave the country defies logic. There were plenty of places to hide in the country, including the Sierra Maestra Mountains. After all, could Batista's troops really surround a whole mountain range?

And who was 'the Revolution' that said it was best for him to leave the country? Fidel? Che? Camilio? Raul? Or perhaps the whole leadership team put the Revolution on hold so that they could convene a leadership meeting and debate what was best for Rafael Bienvenido Cruz Diaz?

Even if they had in fact said he should leave the country, why would such a heroic young man suddenly turn coward and actually leave the country? One would think that Rambo would recharge his cajones and throw himself right back into battle.

Version 2

After I posted a video poking fun at his ridiculous story, Rafael Cruz retooled his story before the OC PAC gathering.

Lie #15b

"When they released me I realized I could not have scrutiny under that condition I could not expose my sister and my parents to that threat. I had no other choice but to leave the country. I had been a straight 'A' student in high school so I figured the easiest way to leave the country was on a student visa. I had always been a straight 'A' student and was accepted by University of Texas and able to get a 4 year student visa."[54]

Suddenly, there are no men on the corners following him 24 x 7? Cuba is a big country. Its population speaks Spanish. It has familiar food. Why did Rafael Cruz feel he had to leave the country? It is likely that all along his parents supported Batista. An education in the US was pretty well reserved for the children of affluent families. Some of those wishful students might have had to earn their way out of the country, a possibility which will be discussed later in Chapter 21.

---

[54] https://youtu.be/h1daylyahdQ

Cuban Commentary: *I was in the mountains with M-26-7. We were able to come and go and conduct raids at that time. – Ernesto, deceased 2014 age 86 (Translated and edited for clarity)*

Chapter 16

Lie # 16a

"So, I figure what's the best way to get out of the country? I know I'll apply to a university in the United States and leave with a student visa."[55]

Several points here:

According to his *National Review Online* interview with Mario Loyola, this occurred in either June or July of 1957[56]. If he had truly spent four years 'in the revolution' committing sabotage, collecting weapons, and spreading propaganda 830 km from home without attending school, how could he think he would be able to get accepted at a US university? For that matter, how did he even know that US institutions of higher education accepted foreign students? And finally how did he come to learn about the existence of the University of Florida (in some speeches he says University of Miami), LSU, and the University of Texas in a week or so?

The internet had not yet been invented, and surely the microfiche films which American students reviewed to learn about colleges and universities were not available in Spanish. Why not go to a school in a Latin country:

---

[55] https://youtu.be/ydVbVBUq6yo
[56] Exile and the Revolution, 11-4-11 Mario Loyola

Spain, Argentina, Chile, Costa Rica, or Uruguay where he would learn in his own language?

Lie # 16b

"I had no other choice but to leave the country. I had been a straight 'A' student in high school so I figured the easiest way to get out of the country was with a student visa." [57]

And lastly, after having been tortured and 'beaten half to death' he was suddenly up and perky enough to think through this strategy and start writing letters requesting acceptance?

Cuban Commentary: *Very privileged. He probably did not attend government schools. He probably attended a Jesuit Academy, like Fidel Castro, where in addition to Spanish he would have also studied Latin and English.- Raul, age 43 (Translated and edited for clarity)*

---

[57] https://youtu.be/ydVbVBUq6yo

Chapter 17

Lie # 17

"I wrote three letters, a letter to the University of Florida, a letter to LSU, and a letter to the University of Texas."[58]

Rafael Bienvenido Cruz Diaz claims that he could not speak a word of English. How could he write letters to three universities that were articulate enough to get him accepted by UT within a few weeks?

He sent no transcript, no statement of family financial condition, just a letter barely two months before school was scheduled to start. (In transit alone via boat and ground transport the letters would have taken one month to go round trip)

Cuban Commentary: *No thought really. You Americans would know better than me if this was possible to occur. - Alfonso, age 83(Translated and edited for clarity)*

---

[58] https://www.youtube.com/watch?v=VsYh_OpbBJO

Chapter 18

Lie # 18

"UT was the first one to assept (sic) me, and that's how I became a Texan."[59]

How did Rafael Cruz write such an amazing letter that so impressed the Admissions Office at the University of Texas causing them to offer him acceptance just a few weeks before the start of the school year?

We are to believe that in the summer of 1957, the University of Texas received a letter from a non-English speaking Cuban boy asking to be admitted for the Fall term, just weeks away. No formal application, just a letter; no financial information; no high school transcript – remember our hero was 830 km away from home for four years. He would have been unable to attend school in Santiago as a young adolescent with no family presence.

Their work being long ago finished to recruit the incoming class of 1961 would UT Admissions personnel have been hanging around campus during the summer months? Hence his application would have had to have been submitted well before the summer of 1957.

---

[59] https://www.youtube.com/watch?v=CkBP9BVaNos

Rafael Bienvenido Cruz Diaz was in fact awarded a Bachelor of Arts Degree on June 3, 1961 from the University of Texas, after having completed eight full semesters of study.[60]

But one last thought: since he was being followed 24/7 by Batista's goons certainly the Batista regime would have been monitoring his family's mail. Wouldn't they have seen the letter from UT, opened it, then dragged Rafael off to the Colonel to put a bullet in his head?

Cuban Commentary: *Good riddance from Cuba. University of Texas and the United States can have this man. - Luis Enrique, age 26 (Translated and edited for clarity)*

---

[60] University of Texas office of the Registrar – Diploma Services

Chapter 19

Lie # 19

"With my letter of acceptance from UT, I went to the American Embassy got a four year student visa."[61]

Student visas have always been issued for one year at a time, renewable if the student continued on their education track.[62] Exceptions have been for post-graduate studies. Surely the two men following him around the clock would have reported back that he was planning to leave the country. The colonel who let him go would have likely had him killed.

The claim of a four year student visa is a slap at undocumented immigrants embroiled in the current immigration debate. Here is what US law says regarding student visas.

Foreign nationals attending college or university in the U.S. have been issued non-immigrant F-1 visas since 1952. They are classified as non-immigrants because their visas are issued with the understanding that they are coming to the country *for the duration of their academic studies.* These regulations were codified in

---

[61] https://www.youtube.com/watch?v=Kf1WkSDcG6c

[62] Immigration and Nationality Act of 1952; affirmed by US State Department Consular Officer (not authorized to be cited)

the Immigration and Nationality Act of 1952. Here is where immigration policy stood in 1957 when Rafael Cruz arrived at college, and for the most part, remains today. Regarding F-1 international students:

Such alien shall establish specifically that he:

(1) *has a residence in a foreign country which he has no intention of abandoning;*

(2) *is a bona fide student qualified to pursue, and is seeking to enter the United States temporarily and solely for the purpose of pursuing, a full course of study;*

(3) *will attend, and has been accepted for attendance by, an established institution of learning or other recognized place of study in the United States; (University of Texas)*

(4) *is in possession of sufficient funds to cover his expenses or other arrangements have been made to provide for his expenses; [Author's note: What few dollars his father could scrounge, or in Ted Cruz's version $100 sewn in his underwear was not sufficient]*
(5) *has sufficient scholastic preparation and knowledge of the English language to enable him to undertake a full course of study in the institution of learning or other place of study by which he has been accepted;* [Author's

note: *"When I arrived my English was limited to Tom is a boy and Mary is a girl."[63] He would have been rejected]* (6) *intends in good faith, and will be able, to depart from the United States upon the termination of student status.*

Since he claims he could not speak a word of English, and all he was going to be traveling with was 'what little dollars his father could scrounge up' Rafael Bienvenido Cruz Diaz would have been denied a visa by the Consular Officer at the US Embassy in Havana. He would never have set foot on a Key West bound ferry.

With all his pontification Rafael Cruz shrugs this visa application process off like it's a mere technicality, like showing your utility bill to get into your local landfill. Well an interview with a US Consular Officer in a US Embassy is a much more deliberate process than that and one which even a skilled con man like Rafael Cruz could not have outsmarted.

Cuban Commentary: *He would have had to go apply for a Cuban Passport and then go to the US Embassy in Havana and apply for a student visa. He would have had an interview and then wait for a reply while the US*

---

[63] https://www.youtube.com/watch?v=9FAwZZ88LTU

Embassy verified his information. This would have taken much time. – Yohandra, lawyer age 33 (Translated and edited for clarity)

Chapter 20

Lie #20

"And then all I needed was a permit to get out of the country. To the equivalent of the FBI or the KGB you could say. And a friend of the family who was a lawyer, he bribed somebody in the government to stamp my (Cuban) passport."[64]

Rafael Cruz previously spoke of a doctor who was a friend of the family and now mentions a lawyer friend of the family. The Cruz Diaz family obviously traveled in upper circles, because Cuba at that time was very status conscious.

Rafael Cruz equates the FBI, a top level law enforcement and investigation agency with the KGB, the Soviet Union's secret police which tracked people and made people disappear? What is wrong with this man's sense of perspective?

When had Rafael Cruz obtained his Cuban passport? Whenever it was that he applied for his Cuban passport, did the two men following him around the clock not report to their superiors that he was applying for a Cuban passport and likely fleeing the country? Wouldn't

---

[64] https://www.youtube.com/watch?v=zPmvC2oux7k

he have been picked up by the Colonel's men and shot in the head?

Cuban Commentary: *There is no surprise that this family of privilege was friendly with lawyers who were also privileged. – Pablo, age 64 (Translated and edited for clarity)*

Chapter 21

Lie #21 (Rafael Cruz's revised version of his Lie #20)

In an April, 2015 CBN video Rafael Cruz claims that he 'convinced the Cuban government to let him leave the country on a student visa.[65]

So Rafael Cruz changes another portion of his story. His story went from the bribing lawyer to his convincing the government to let him go. No longer did the lawyer friend of the family have to bribe a government official for him to go. This reinforces the theory held by several Cuban acquaintances that Rafael Cruz was involved in the torture and murder of William Soler and three other 14 year olds on January 2, 1957.[66]

They believe that Rafael Cruz 'earned' his exit from the country by spying on and informing on 'alleged revolutionaries.' Or perhaps Rafael Cruz can explain how one convinced the oppressive, military dictatorship that controlled the Cuban government which had jailed and tortured him and had followed him 24/7 to let him leave the country on a student visa.

---

[65] https://www.youtube.com/watch?v=B5f6-WntDSw
[66] William Soler - Chapter 88

Cuban Commentary: *He is a comedian. He went to Havana and the Presidential Palace and asked Mr. Batista please let me go to university in United States? There was no restriction on leaving the country at this time but maybe there was for rich young boys who wanted to go to school in the United States. I do not know; my family was not wealthy like the Cruz Diaz family. So he might have had to earn his departure by turning spy for the Batista Regime. – Luis Enrique, age 26 (Translated and edited for clarity)*

Chapter 22

Lie # 22

"So one morning with the car in the garage of my father's house I laid on the floor of the back seat – my father drove to Havana, and I boardered (sic), boarded a ferryboat to Key West." [67]

When he went for both his Cuban passport and US Visa the two men following him would have been aware he was leaving Cuba for the US. So why would he have to lie down on the floor of his father's car? He was going to have to deal with Cuban immigration when he got to the ferry dock anyway. Oh wait, he convinced the Batista government to let him leave the country, so why the need to lie on the floor? One would expect the Batista Regime might send an emissary to the ferry dock to wish him well.

Very few homes in Cuba had garages. These were the homes of the elite. If the Cruz Diaz family did have a garage it would have put them among the elite in Matanzas. View photograph #2 on page 185 and judge if that person could have hidden crouched down in the back seat of a car. And if he had really 'convinced the Cuban

---

[67] https://www.youtube.com/watch?v=3WbA9s61kHI

government' to let him leave the country on a student visa, why would he have to hide?

Cuban Commentary: *A home with a garage? Wealthy Cuban family. – Elgis, age 62 (Translated and edited for clarity)*

Chapter 23

Lie # 23

"Landed in Key West with nothing but a few dollars sewn into my underwear; my mother was afraid they were gonna steal my money, what few dollars that my father was able to scrounge that she sewed a pocket in my underwear. And I only had enough money for my bus fare to Austin and maybe to eat a couple of hamburgers along the way. My mother was afraid my money might get stolen so she sewed a pocket in my underwear."[68]

His parents were affluent; the father earned $300 a month as a salesman for RCA; the mother earned $140 per month as a public school teacher. Their annual income was 13 times the Cuban national average, and his father Rafael Bienvenido could only 'scrounge up a few dollars?'

Being from Cuba where rice, beans, and pork were the staple, how did he know what hamburgers were?

Since he was headed to Austin, Texas why take a ferry to Key West. Ferry service was also available to New Orleans and to Texas City, Texas just south of Houston, both in much closer proximity to Austin than

---

[68] https://www.youtube.com/watch?v=m5hPEE6mWUw

Key West. With respect to his mother worrying that he would get robbed, view photo #2 on page 185.

Does this look like a person who would worry about being robbed on the ferry? He claims he spent four years as a revolutionary; that he was later beaten and tortured. Wouldn't he be a tough guy? Other passengers might have been fearful of him due to his appearance; he might have looked like a terrorist. Someone who spent four years fighting a revolution and was jailed and tortured should not have been worried about possibly losing the 'few dollars his father could scrounge up.'

Finally, there certainly must have been security officers on the ferry. He could have sat by them to keep his money safe or his affluent family could have booked him a private cabin on the ferry.

When he landed in Key West, US Immigration officials would have questioned him as to his financial resources to sustain himself as a student in the US. They would have also realized that his English skills were limited to 'Tom is a boy, Carol is a girl'. Both matters would have caused him to be flagged and detained and eventually returned to Cuba.

The ferry (actually more like a small cruise ship with staterooms) from Havana docks at the pier in Key West. Passengers disembark with their belongings and head into the immigration reception area. US Citizens proceed to the left, all others to the right.

Imagine how the conversation might have gone:

(It would have taken place in Spanish but it will be presented in Rafael Cruz English here)

Immigration agent: *Welcome to the United States*

Rafael: *Oh, tank you berry berry much.*

Agent: *And what is the nature of your visit?*

Rafael: *I am going to Austeen (sic) Texas to go to University of Texas*

Agent: *How many suitcases are you declaring?*

Rafael: *None*

Agent: *You have no clothes?*

Rafael: *Oh yes, sir. I have my chirt, my ponts, my socks, my choos, and my underwear with the Mommy pocket sewn in.*

Agent: *That's all the clothes you have?*

Rafael: *Jes sir.*

Agent: *Do you have any money? Hey, you can't pull down your pants in here!*

Rafael: *Sir, I show you. My mother she sew a pocket in the back of my underwear to keep my money safe.*

Agent: *How much do you have?*

Rafael: *$100.*

Agent: *US law requires a student coming in on an F-1 Visa to be able to speak English and to have financial resources for a full year. How on earth did you get the consular officer in Havana to give you a visa?*

Rafael: *A friend of the family who is a lawyer bribed someone for me to get the visa.*

Agent: *I'm sorry but you cannot enter the US. You have only the clothes on your back and some cash tucked down there by your buttocks. You don't meet the requirements.*

Rafael: *But sir you don't understand. My son Ted who will be born in Canada will run for President of the United States in 58 years. Ted has to be able to say 'my father came from Cuba with just the clothes on his back and $100 in his underwear'. We will have to look like We the People.*

Agent: *Hey Murphy, we got a real piker here. Cuff him and take him over to departures. He's going back to Havana. Oh, before you cuff both wrists have him slide his hand down his underwear and pull out $20 for a ferry ticket home.*

Chapter 24

Lie # 24

"When he landed in Austin, Texas in 1957 he was 18 and he couldn't speak a word of English. He had $100 sewn into his underwear." Ted Cruz – Hillsdale College Commencement 2014 [69]

Here is an example of Ted Cruz embellishing his father's lie. He increases the 'few dollars the father could scrounge for bus fare and a few hamburgers along the way' up to $100. And this is no doubt designed to make people feel sorry for Rafael that all he had to his name was $100.

That $100 in 1957 would be worth $850.76 today in 2015; how many college students would be thrilled to arrive at college their first day with that kind of cash in their underwear?

On another point, did Rafael Cruz wear the same pair of underwear the entire journey? Traveling on the ferry, up through the Florida Keys, likely having a layover in Miami, up to the Panhandle, across the Gulf Coast all the way to Texas with perhaps some layovers along the way in the August heat and humidity would

---

[69] https://www.youtube.com/watch?v=izU7sH-0T_E

certainly have ripened the underwear and probably put quite a stench on his cash.

Ted Cruz regularly uses the phrase 'when he landed in Austin.' Is this a slip of the tongue from one of the lying duo? In 1957 Eastern Airlines offered scheduled daily service between Havana, Cuba and Austin, Texas with a brief stopover in Miami.[70] Could it be that Rafael Bienvenido Cruz Diaz, son of an affluent Cuban family did not travel to the US by ferry but flew to Austin on Eastern Airlines? After all, if he had truly gone to the Port in Havana he would have realized he had two better options to get to Austin, Texas – a ferry to New Orleans or a ferry to Texas City. Texas.[71]

Overarching Ted Cruz's lie here is the fact that with no ability to speak English and only a few dollars or $100 sewn in his underwear, Rafael Bienvenido Cruz Diaz would never have been granted a student visa by the US State Department Consular Officer.

I have personal knowledge of someone being admitted to the United States with only $100. My grandfather Theodore LeBon and his brother arrived from Belgium in the Port of Boston aboard the MV Saxony on February 1, 1906. The ship's manifest showed that

---

[70] Eastern Airlines flight timetables
[71] http://en.wikipedia.org/wiki/West_India_Fruit_and_Steamship_Company

between them they had $100[72]. Unlike Rafael Cruz they were here to work full time in textile mills that had been built by Belgian industrialists. And unlike Rafael and Ted Cruz my grandfather and his brother were men of honesty and integrity.

It's amazing that Ted Cruz, the legal 'whiz kid' who has argued successfully before the US Supreme Court as Solicitor General of the State of Texas never thought to review Immigration Law before he and his Daddy concocted these lies to hoodwink Evangelical voters and Tea Party members. Taking that one step further, it's amazing how gullible Evangelicals and Tea Party people can be. Drop a few Bible verses, tell a wild near death story with intervention by God, and they will buy whatever you are selling.

---

[72] Obtained copy of manifest through Ancestry.com

Chapter 25

Lie # 25

"Got to Austin, went straight to the University Office of Student Affairs and I said 'well here I am', it was a month before school started and I said 'well I need a job, I don't have any money'. Well, within 24 hours they sent me to the IRS . . . the INS, and within 24 hours I had a Social Security number – a valid legal Social Security number And because well I needed to work to pay for my university.

I couldn't speak a word of English so the obvious job was being a 'deeshwasher' . . . you don't have to talk to anybody to wash 'deeshes'. So I got a job as a deeshwasher; worked full time, went to school full time and paid for my school."[73]

How did Rafael Cruz Diaz obtain a Social Security number, he was a foreign national here on a student visa? How would he have been handed a Social Security card on the spot at the Immigration and Naturalization Service office? Social Security cards have always been issued by the Social Security Administration and they have never been handed out, they have always

---

[73] https://www.youtube.com/watch?v=pHF4b6HQ8TU

been mailed. How did he even know how the American system worked, and that he might be able to secure a job when he arrived in Austin?

Did UT staff speak Spanish in 1957? Who translated for him in the Office of Student Affairs? UT let a Cuban national with no ties in the US who could not speak a word of English and who had no financial support enroll in and attend classes, live in a dorm, and eat from the food plan 'on credit' – very doubtful. The 'valid legal Social Security number' line is a slap at today's undocumented immigrants and one that he delivers with a flourish and usually draws applause.

Social Security number weren't used for federal tax purposes when Rafael Cruz arrived in 1957, this would not begin until 1961. In 1957, it was a way to keep track of the earnings history of U.S. workers for Social Security entitlement and benefit computation purposes which Rafael Cruz would not have been entitled to.

Why did he even have to work to pay for his school? The tuition at UT was $270 a semester in 1970 for an out-of-state student[74], so it had to have been less in 1957. His parents in Cuba had a combined monthly

---

[74] UT Tuition Chart - appendix

income of $440. Three weeks of Mama and Papa Cruz Diaz's income would pay for the semester.

Let's cut right to the quick in this lie: Had he showed up at the Student Affairs Office at the University of Texas in Austin and said, "Necesito un trabajo; no tengo dinero" (I need a job, I have no money) and there had been someone in the building to translate (remember this was 1957) the office of student affairs would have done what the law required them to do and immediately contacted the Immigration and Naturalization Service. They would have said, "Hey, we have a young man here from Cuba who wants to be admitted to the University, but he claims he is penniless and only has the clothes on his back."

The INS would have immediately sent agents to UT to take Rafael Bienvenido Cruz Diaz into custody and charged him with fraud and begun deportation proceedings. He would have been deported to Cuba and as someone who had a visa revoked due to fraud would never have been allowed to immigrate to the US during the Castro years.

The fact is Rafael Bienvenido Cruz Diaz came from an affluent Cuban family. The parents combined annual income was $5,280. This was 13 times the Median

Family Income in Cuba in 1957 which was $400 annually.

To put this in perspective using contemporary numbers the Median Annual Family income in the United States in 2013 was $51,939 dollars. Thirteen times that is $675,207 which would put a family in the top .5% income bracket.

I'm not a lawyer. I'm a 58 year old former sales trainer who was forced to retire when diagnosed with Early Onset Alzheimer's in 2012. I'm up against a man regarded as one of the brightest lawyers in the country, the former Solicitor General for the State of Texas, a man who has argued before the US Supreme Court nine times.

So in order to hopefully head off any legal mumbo jumbo about Immigration Law in 1957 or new lies by Ted Cruz I am presenting a *Findings of Fact, Conclusion of Law, and Order* entered in an Immigration Appeal Hearing held in 1959 regarding a Chinese student. The student had been ordered deported because he misrepresented his financial condition when he applied for an F-1 visa to come study in the US.

The record contains a great deal of legalese. If you don't want to read it all you can read the salient points which I bolded in the text as well as author notes.

Here is the full text of the case:

In the matter of C. S. L., A Chinese citizen In Deportation Proceedings A-11132697

Decided by Board eh-III-e October 15, *1959*

Misrepresentation—by nonimmigrant student as to finances is within section 212(a)(19) of 1952 act. **A nonimmigrant student who represented in his visa application that he had sufficient funds to finance his education in the United States when in fact he had only his passage money was clearly not qualified for student status at the time he applied for his nonimmigrant visa. Hence, his misrepresentation was a violation of section 212(a) (19) of the act and he is deportable** under section 241(a) (1). (Cf. *Matter of S C ,* 7 I. & N. Dec. 76, and *Matter of C—T P ,* A-10344385, Int. Dec. No. 953.)

CHARGE

Order: Immigration and Nationality Act of 1952—Section 241(a) (1) [8 U.S.C. 1251(a) (1)1—Excludable at entry as an alien who obtained a visa by fraud or willfully misrepresenting a material fact, contrary to section 212(a) i19) 1.8 U.S.C. 1182 (a) (19)].

BEFORE THE BOARD

Discussion: This case is before us on appeal from a decision of the special inquiry officer, dated March 24, 1959, holding the alien deportable and denying voluntary departure.

Respondent, a 31-yearold native and citizen of China, last entered the United States at Seattle, Washington, on June 16, 1957, as a nonimmigrant student for a period of one year. [*Author's note: non-immigrant F-1 visas have always been granted for one year and renewed each subsequent school year that the student matriculated. Rafael Cruz could not have obtained a 4 year visa as he claims in Chapter 19*] At that time he presented a non-quota immigrant visa issued by the American Consulate at Taipei, Taiwan (Formosa).

The charge arose as a result of certain false statements concerning respondent's financial responsibility, made in connection with his visa application. Respondent described himself as "self-financed" and on the back of Certificate of Acceptance by the University of Michigan, it was stated that he had $3200 on deposit in banks in the United States. This information was supported by written statements to the same effect from four American banks.

Respondent later stated that he 'borrowed' the sums of money from four friends in the United States, although promptly after the record of deposits were made he endorsed withdrawal slips back to the 'lenders.' As an actual fact, respondent had only money to cover his transportation to the United States and upon arrival immediately began working to pay his first semester's tuition. Thereafter, **on November 4, 1957, respondent received Immigration Service permission to work a maximum of 20 hours per week and has since**

maintained himself. [Author's note: special exceptions were granted by INS for foreign students to work but the limit was 20 hours per week. Note also the thoroughness of INS investigators; they obtained this student's bank records]

The special inquiry officer held that since sufficient funds to finance a student in the United States is a requirement for the issuance of a non-quota immigrant student's visa (22 CFR 41.81(a) (4)) and respondent gave false information that he was self-sustaining, respondent's statements constituted a willful misrepresentation of his assets. As to whether these statements were material, the special inquiry officer stated:

The State Department regulation is clear cut and emphatic in its language requiring a showing of assets sufficient to defray the costs of a temporary stay in the United States while pursuing an education. *[Author's note: clear cut and emphatic – could not have said it better myself]* To construe this requirement as satisfied by someone in respondent's circumstances would obfuscate, if not extirpate, the true meaning and purpose of the regulation.

Hence, it is found that the respondent's misrepresentation concealed facts which 'might well have prompted a final refusal of the visa. It is concluded that he is subject to deportation as charged in the order to show cause by reason of his willful misrepresentation of a material fact in the procurement of his nonimmigrant student visa.

Concerning respondent's request for voluntary departure, the special inquiry officer felt that although there was no question of respondent's earnestness in seeking a higher education in the United States, 'the means respondent used to effectuate his purpose cannot be condoned' in the light of the deceit practiced upon the American consul. The special inquiry officer also felt that respondent in his various statements to the Immigration Service spoke in half-truths and equivocation. For these reasons, the special inquiry officer concluded that respondent lacked the good moral character required and was, consequently, statutorily ineligible for discretionary relief in the form of voluntary departure. However, even if considered eligible for this relief, the special inquiry officer concluded that the same reasons were 'sufficiently derogatory to justify denial.'

Counsel contends that the record fails to establish that a ground of inadmissibility probably existed (rather than a mere possibility of such inadmissibility) at the time respondent made the false statements in connection with his visa application/
On the other hand, the Immigrant Service contends that respondent was not an eligible non-immigrant student [section 101(a) (15) 395 (F), (26)] at the time he applied for a nonimmigrant visa, in the light of the requirements of 22 CFR 41.81(a) (4), requiring that he have sufficient funds in his possession to cover his expenses while in the United States as a student or that other appropriate arrangements have been

made to provide for these expenses, and, therefore, respondent's concealment was fatal as a violation of section 212(a) (19).

Hence, the question turns on whether respondent was entitled by law to enter the United States as a nonimmigrant student had the true facts been revealed. According to 22 CFR 41.81 (Burden of proof and evidence of student status), an alien applying for a visa as a nonimmigrant under the provisions of section 101(a) (15) (F) of the act shall not only have the burden of establishing that he is entitled to classification as a student within the meaning of that section of the act, but also that he is not ineligible to receive a visa as a nonimmigrant and is specifically required to establish, among other things, that "he is in possession of sufficient funds to cover his expenses" [(a) (4)].

Since respondent was not in possession of cash, neither in the hand nor in the bank, sufficient to cover his expenses while in this country and other arrangements not having been made, he was clearly unqualified for student status at the time he applied for his nonimmigrant visa. Hence, respondent's false representation of the facts relevant to his right to obtain a visa constituted misrepresentation of a material fact and a violation of section 21:2(a) (10). Because respondent's counsel has not contested the special inquiry officer's conclusion of ineligibility for voluntary departure and denial of this relief, we will affirm this conclusion in the light of all the surrounding facts. Deportability is supported and the appeal must be dismissed.

Order: **IT IS HEREBY ORDERED THAT THE APPEAL BE DISMISSED AND RESPONDENT REMANDED FOR DEPORTATION TO HIS HOME COUNTRY**

The Rafael Cruz liarpalooza shows Rafael Cruz not only to be a fraud, a liar, and a con man, but someone who will steal anyone's honor to try to prove his manhood. While he and Ted laugh all the way to the ballot box, once again this despicable man steals someone's honor.

'Arrived in Key West from Cuba with just the clothes on his back and a few dollars.' Why does that sound familiar? Because it's the narrative of many brave Cubans who have headed to their shores under cover of night, boarded all manner of watercraft made from all sorts of materials and floated on a keel and a prayer across the Straits of Florida for several days hoping to reach Key West. In his lies of revolutionary heroics Rafael Cruz steals the valor of Fidel Castro and Frank Pais. In this lie he steals the valor of the many courageous Cubans, those who made it and those who didn't, with just the clothes on their back.

Chapter 26

Lie #26

"I couldn't speak a word of English."[75]

How did Rafael Cruz navigate his travel on the ferry? How did he figure out the bus schedule to Austin? How did he read menus? Where did he stay when he arrived in Austin since the dorms would not have been open for a month? How did he manage his studies since everything was in English? When the Office of Student Affairs sent him (supposedly) to the INS, how did he communicate with the personnel there? Why did he not go to a university in Latin America or Spain where Spanish was the spoken language?

---

[75] https://www.youtube.com/watch?v=9FAwZZ88LTU

Chapter 27

Lie #27

"But he went and got a job washing dishes; he made 50 cents an hour, and he worked seven days a week and paid his way through the University of Texas and then he graduated and got a job and started a small business and then went on to work toward the American dream. Now imagine if the minimum wage had been $2 an hour instead of being able to work for 50 cents; he might never have had that opportunity to get that first job and work through school, and work towards the American dream." Ted Cruz Hillsdale College Commencement 2014[76]

In 1957 the U.S. Minimum wage was $1.00 per hour. Rafael Cruz could not have been in possession of a Social Security card, and he worked for half the minimum wage. If he had been granted a work permit by the INS (very rare for a freshman) he would have been limited to working 20 hours per week. He would not have been able to work full time, seven days a week. He was way ahead of his time but he was what Ted Cruz, Sarah Palin, Michele Bachmann, Louie Gohmert and all the

---

[76] https://www.youtube.com/watch?v=Z4att1RlqvQ

other right wing Republicans and Tea Party zealots call a 'job stealing illegal alien'. Rafael Cruz was violating federal laws and was in fact an illegal immigrant!

Rafael Cruz stole a job from a hard working American who probably needed a job to support his family. Rafael Cruz violated the law, Rafael Cruz was a criminal. Rafael Cruz should have been arrested and deported.

If he wants to claim that he actually had legal documented wages in 1957, let him present Social Security statements.

'Went on to work towards the American dream.' The life Raphael Cruz created was more nightmare than dream for the two wives and three children he abandoned and it will be covered in detail later in this book. Of course he and Ted would eventually snag a US Senate seat and set their eyes on the White House. How many lives have been and will be disrupted throughout this odyssey? They will likely just be written off as collateral damage.

Chapter 28

Lie # 28

"At that time you would get all your food for free, so I would eat enough in my eight hours of work to not be hungry the other 16. I didn't have any money to buy food."[77]

Wasn't there a meal plan at UT? Ask a dietitian for an opinion. Eight hours eating at the restaurant; say 2:00 – 10:00 pm; sleeping, getting up, and sitting in class all day without breakfast or lunch would cause problems with concentration and cause severe weight loss. Rafael Cruz is a human, not a chipmunk. He couldn't store food in his cheeks. Whatever he ate would be digested and he would be hungry a short time later.

There is a current diet fad called the *8 Hour Diet.* It claims that if you consume all your food in an eight hour span every day you will lose 5 pounds per week. Rafael Cruz would have withered away to nothing. According to a Noelani Holmes a senior in the Nutrition Program at Texas Woman's University[78] the starches

---

[77] https://www.youtube.com/watch?v=nHK3B_RJDKU

[78] Noelani Holmes, Texas Woman's University Nutrition, Class of 2016

from the restaurant food would have overwhelmed his metabolism and made school a serious challenge because the concept of healthy eating did not exist in 1957.

If he had in fact obtained a work permit from the INS he would have been limited to 20 hours per week. That would have been at best 3-4 days working. Where would he have fed himself the other days? Out of the swill buckets behind the restaurant?

I too worked as a dishwasher as a 15 year old, at Kim's Kitchen in Bellingham, Massachusetts. Yes I got my food for free, but it was one meal per shift. Rafael Cruz implies that at the restaurant he has never named publicly where he claimed to have worked there was an all-you-can-eat buffet for the employees. How ridiculous.

Chapter 29

Lie # 29

"I took the advice of my English teacher in Cuba. I would sit in a movie theater watch the movie three times over – taught myself English in one month."[79]

Thirty days? My *English as a Second Language* (ESL)[80] students take a couple of years, and they work hard at it using workbooks, class time, group exercises, practice, etc. Sitting in a movie theater watching the same movie over and over again only makes you a parrot.

You cannot learn the English language from a movie; the dialogue is very limited. To learn the English language you have to understand how to form sentences (especially flipping adjectives and nouns from Spanish dialect – casa roja = red house) how to conjugate verbs, and other language skills.

Even now 58 years later Rafael Cruz sounds like he just got off the boat. Sitting in a movie theater and watching replays would only have allowed him to parrot words, and not understand their meaning.

---

[79] https://www.youtube.com/watch?v=wVLd0MgCBdo
[80] Volunteer teacher for LIFT – Literary Instruction for Texas

If he had an English teacher in Cuba, how could it be that he arrived not being able to speak one word of English? Then again how did he make it through his interview with the US Consular Officer for a student visa? Did the English teacher go along and act as a ventriloquist? This lie is another slap at today's immigrants; the implication is, 'why can't they learn to speak English, I did it in 30 days?'

Cuban Commentary: *Of course he had an English teacher. The Jesuit academies stressed languages. And he certainly left Cuba speaking English. – Alfonso, age 83 (Translated and edited for clarity)*

Chapter 30

Lie # 30

"At the start of 1958 I began speaking to Rotary Clubs around Austin in favor of Castro."[81]

Rafael Cruz claims he arrived in the country not able to speak a word of English. He watched movies for 30 days and claims he learned the entire English language. Four months later an 18 year old Cuban dishwasher who likely didn't own a suit is addressing the white-bread Rotary Clubs around Austin? What interest would they possibly have in Fidel Castro? Why would they want to hear it from a teen aged dishwasher? How would Raphael Cruz have gotten himself around to the various Rotary Club meetings? How did he balance his class schedule since most Rotary Club meetings were at Noon? How did he even know what Rotary Clubs were, and how did he reach out to them to arrange his speaking engagements?

He talks in his speeches about Ted at 12 years old being part of a group called the Constitutional Collaborators – they would attend Rotary Clubs meetings to show off their skills of having memorized the US

---

[81] https://www.youtube.com/watch?v=Q48IhT5cd2U

Constitution. That is probably what gave Rafael Cruz the idea to claim he went around talking to Rotary Clubs, performing vicariously through his son Ted.

Chapter 31

Lie # 31

"I went back to Cuba in the summer of 1959 and I got the shock of my life. This same man who had talked about hope and change was now talking about how the rich were evil, how they oppressed the poor and the need to redistribute the wealth. He confiscated property, shut down newspapers, forbade religious practice, and arrested priests."[82]

Who paid for the trip, since he was a 50 cent an hour dishwasher? Did he hear this talk from Castro for the first time when he arrived in Cuba? He received the shock of his life? Why hadn't his parents told him of all these supposed changes? This is another attempt to intertwine Castro and Obama with words from the 2008 campaign. Why doesn't Rafael Cruz recruit Joe the Plumber or Sean Hannity to help pitch this tale?

Six months after the success of the Revolution nothing had really changed yet except one – on May 17 Fidel Castro signed the Agrarian Reform Act, expropriating over 1,000 acres of farmland that had been owned by foreign entities. In fact things would not begin

---

[82] https://www.youtube.com/watch?v=1krQo2FGGA4

to change until President Eisenhower started antagonizing Cuba by signing a covert action plan on March 17, 1960.

Rafael Cruz states that in five short months Castro had banned religion, free press, the right of assembly and forced his father to give up his high paying job as a salesman for RCA and become a fisherman. Rafael Cruz claims his father was forced to give his daily catch to the government. His mother a 6th grade teacher was forced to teach Marxism in schools and depending on which version of the story you believe she either faked an attack of insanity and a doctor friend of the family gave her a fake diagnosis, or she refused to teach Marxism and was fired.

Castro did eventually implement those policies but that was long after Rafael Cruz would have returned to Austin and around the time he got a young woman pregnant out of wedlock.

Rafael Cruz claims that when he returned to Austin in June of 1959 he went back to all those Rotary Clubs and gave speeches decrying Castro. More broken English about Fidel Castro from the dishwasher, just what Rotary Clubs lived for, right?

It is very likely that the tale of visiting Cuba in the summer of 1959 is a bald faced lie and that Rafael Cruz has never returned to Cuba since August of 1957. Had he returned home from the US in 1959, he would have been prohibited from leaving Cuba and returning to the US by the Castro government.

A search of old dusty boxes of arrival/departure records for the Port of Havana shows no Rafael Bienvenido Cruz Diaz arriving or departing during the period May 15, 1959 to July 15, 1959.[83]

Cuban Commentary: *None of these things occurred by June of 1959. If he had really returned to Cuba having 20 years of age he would not have been allowed to leave. He would have been conscripted to the military because Fidel was worried that the United States might invade and he wanted to increase the number of soldiers. His parents would have warned him not to come back, I believe. Alfonso, age 83(Translated and edited for clarity)*

---

[83] Cuban records search, December, 2014

Chapter 32

Lie #32

"Castro ordered teachers to teach Marxism and Leninism in schools. My mother was a public school teacher and she would not teach this, so she faked an attack of insanity. She was running up and down the halls of her school, pulling her hair, screaming, foaming at the mouth. A friend of the family who was a doctor wrote her a fake diagnosis and she was dismissed from her job for reason of mental illness."[84]

When I saw the videos of this I could not stop laughing. In front of an outdoor Tea Party Rally in Dallas emceed by talk radio host Mark Davis and at a Freedom Works gathering organized by anti-Muslim bigot Katrina Pierson, Rafael Cruz told this ridiculous story about a faked attack of insanity and his gullible followers ate it up.

In early 2013 I wrote a post on my blog about Rafael Cruz's mother's fake insanity and I posted a link to it on his Facebook page. His allegedly evangelical christian (intentional lower case 'c') followers came after me with vitriolic fervor both on Rafael Cruz's Facebook

---

[84] https://www.youtube.com/watch?v=VcYme2KSRmg

page and the Comments section on my Blog. Fortunately all comments posted to my Blog are subject to approval.

My ridicule of his insanity tale got me blocked from Rafael Cruz's Facebook page. But it did have an impact. On July 5, 2013 Rafael Cruz was in Salt Lake City to address a rally sponsored by Freedom Works, a conservative voter's activist club. He gave his usual carnival barker routine and when he got to his mother's work situation he stated that '*she refused to teach Marxism and she was fired.*' Finally Mother Cruz can rest in peace; she is no longer insane, though the same cannot be said about her son.

It would be 17 months after Rafael Cruz's alleged visit home to Cuba that Fidel Castro would declare himself a Marxist-Leninist on December 2, 1961, but that ideology was not introduced into schools until much later, and only in the upper grades.

If Rafael Cruz's mother did in fact lose her teaching job it was probably due to racism. On January 1, 1961 Fidel Castro kicked off Cuba's National Literacy Campaign. He closed the public schools in the cities and ordered the teachers to go into the country and teach the peasants to read and write. The peasants were mostly black and many white teachers refused this assignment and were terminated. It's more likely that is why Rafael Cruz's mother lost her employment as a teacher.

Cuban Commentary: *The talk of Marxism did not arrive for several years. His mother living in a beautiful home would not have wanted to go to the farms and teach black people. – Ernesto, deceased 2014 age 86 (Translated and edited for clarity)*

Chapter 33

Lie # 33

"I remember when the soldiers used to come into the classrooms and tell the children to put their heads on the desk and pray to God for candy. Then raise their heads and look – no candy. Now put your heads down and pray to Fidel for candy. The soldiers would sneak around the classroom and put candy on the desks. Then say, look children Fidel gave you candy"[85].

How does he remember that? Was he there? I've talked to Cuban residents in their 60's and no one remembers that. Once again Rafael Cruz changes a portion of his story.

In other speeches he remembered that his mother told him – hadn't his mother left teaching because she was insane or fired? And in the version Ted Cruz tells AM660 Talk Radio Host John David Wells, Ted Cruz claims the soldiers came into the class brandishing machine guns, which drew an 'Oh My' from Wells.

Cuban Commentary: *I never got any candy from Fidel or the soldiers. Maybe before he dies I should go visit Fidel*

---

[85] https://www.youtube.com/watch?v=4A7EdCG5rQs

and ask for my candy? – Pablo, age 64 (Translated and edited for clarity)

Chapter 34

Lie # 34

"I graduated from college in 3 ½ years."[86]

He enrolled at the University of Texas in September, 1957 and he graduated with a degree in Mathematics June 3, 1961. - Per University of Texas Office of the Registrar. That would be four years, but as previously noted his math skills leave something to be desired, as does his honesty. Rafael Cruz has this deep need to be superior at everything he does. Perhaps he suffers from some type of male deficiency syndrome?

---

[86] https://www.youtube.com/watch?v=4mdrUsFVSTA

Chapter 35

Lie # 35

"Two times I should have been killed and I escaped
death. God had other plans for my life."[87]

Rafael Cruz got his girlfriend pregnant in college.
Then 359 days later he had his second child. He
abandoned his wife and two daughters and took up with
another woman. He and the woman moved to Calgary
where they had a son Ted in 1970. Three years later he
abandoned the two of them in Canada and returned to
Texas. Those were God's plans for his life? Sounds more
like Satan's plan.

Cuban Commentary: *A miracle man – he escaped*
Batista's bullets twice! Maybe he walked on the ocean
from Havana to Key West. – Yohandra, age 33
(Translated and edited for clarity)

---

[87] https://www.youtube.com/watch?v=ktyx_7-JRcc

Chapter 36

Lie # 36

"Yes, I knew Frank Pais; I was in Santiago when Castro was supposed to come from Mexico. (On November 30, 1956) We were divided into two groups; Frank Pais led one and I was with the other. "[88] (Rafael Cruz's response to a question I posed to him at a Weatherford, TX Tea Party meeting in 2013)

Actually the group of 300 students had been organized and trained by Frank Pais and they wore the olive 26th of July Movement uniforms with red and black armbands. They were separated into three groups, not two, and they had three targets – the Custom Houses, the Harbormaster's Office, and the Police Station.

Rafael Bienvenido Cruz Diaz's name is conspicuously absent from the list of hero/participants of this event that is posted in the two Museums of the Revolution – the Moncada Barracks in Santiago and the former Presidential Palace in Havana. Nor is there a school, hospital, or other public building in Cuba named after Rafael Bienvenido Cruz Diaz. Every public building in Cuba is named after a Cuban hero such as Frank Pais,

---

[88] https://www.youtube.com/watch?v=kmmtNE2DNT8

William Soler, and Jose Marti among others, but not
Rafael Bienvenido Cruz Diaz.

In an article by Rafael Cruz's fellow Cuban-
American Mario Loyola in *National Review Online*[89],
Cruz had given Loyola a different story:
*"They knew that Castro intended to land in Cuba and
hoped to organize an urban uprising along with it. But
Castro and the anti-Batista forces failed to coordinate in
any meaningful way, and when Castro's boat landed near
Manzanillo in Oriente province, the hoped-for urban
uprising failed to materialize."*

So to a fellow Cuban-American who might
actually know the truth, Rafael Cruz downplays his
involvement in the fight during Castro's arrival. But to a
group of fawning, gullible Texas Tea Party members, he
is Rambo. Here is what *Time Magazine* reported in its
December 10, 1956 issue:

*"Just before dawn one day last week, the revolt got under
way—again in Santiago. Machine gunners, in olive-drab
uniforms with black-and-red armbands marked "26 de
julio," fired on police headquarters.*

---

[89] Exile and the Revolution, 11-4-11 Mario Loyola

"At the same time they tossed grenades and gasoline bombs on the building from a nearby rooftop and burned it down, while ammunition popped inside. For a time the attackers roamed the area freely, looting a hardware store for weapons."

Rafael Cruz often says – when speaking about President Obama and 'all his lies' that Marxists will say whatever just to advance their cause. Rafael Cruz would certainly qualify as a Marxist under that definition.

Cuban Commentary: *Shame on him for putting himself on the level of Frank Pais, a genuine and beloved hero. This man will burn with the Devil. – Yaneli, age 46 (Translated and edited for clarity)*

Author's Note: I had learned of this appearance by Rafael Cruz before the Parker County Tea Party in Weatherford, TX via a story in a local newspaper which came up in a Google search. When I rose to ask a question and mentioned that I had been to Cuba on numerous Mission trips Rafael Cruz looked like he was going to wet his pants. His answer to my question was made up as he went along which is apparent watching the video. This was the last time ever that a Rafael Cruz local appearance was noted in the media. I did learn of an appearance in Florida and an acquaintance Tracey Eaton who

had *been Dallas Morning News* Havana Bureau Chief attended
and sought to interview Rafael Cruz afterwards. Cruz refused.
He obviously will only speak to media like the Christian
Broadcasting Network which has fallen for his bogus life tale.

Chapter 37

Lie # 37

"The day Frank Pais was killed I should have been killed too. . . . It was just by the Grace of God that I wasn't killed, because God had other plans for my life."[90]

Rafael Cruz falsely claims that Frank Pais was killed in Santiago in December, 1956 because Rafael Cruz was not there, it is all a lie. Frank Pais was killed on July 30, 1957, seven months after Rafael Cruz claimed, and just days before Rafael Cruz left for the United States. Frank Pais' funeral was held the day after he was tortured and shot on the street in Santiago by Police Chief Colonel Jose Salas Canizares A throng of 60,000 people turned out for his funeral. The crowd was so unmanageable that the police shut down access to the city.

This is another proclamation in which Rafael Cruz claims God saved him from death because God had other plans for his life. It is reprehensible the assertions that Rafael Cruz makes with these two lies: first, he again seeks to steal someone else's valor by fabricating a story that elevates him to the level of a national hero. Second

---

[90] https://www.youtube.com/watch?v=37lfZFchels

he implies that his life was more important to God than was Frank Pais' life.

As an afterthought to Chapter 14 where Rafael Cruz claims that a woman from the underground told him the Revolution said he had to leave the country, if Rafael Cruz were such a heroic figure, would a 'Revolution' that barely had 300 fighters have sent him out of the country? No, they would have gotten him to the mountains or to a safe place somewhere in Cuba.

Cuban Commentary: *Frank Pais escaped and then was captured and killed during July. He was not killed in December in Santiago. Shame again on this man Rafael Cruz. It is a sad thing that he was not killed that day. – Luis Enrique, age 26 (Translated and edited for clarity)*

Chapter 38

Lie # 38

At the Weatherford Tea Party meeting I asked Rafael Cruz off camera after the event – "Do you still have your uniform from the battle in Santiago?" *"We didn't have uniforms; Castro's people never had uniforms, they were rebels. ('they', not' we') Without a uniform it was easier to blend in. The soldiers and police had uniforms."[91]*

Frank Pais had designed a uniform for the members of FEU (Federation of University Students); it was olive with red and black arm bands. They were sewn secretly at night by women workers from the garment factory in their homes. All 300 university students who participated in the battle when Castro returned from Mexico wore these M 26-7 uniforms.

Had Rafael Cruz been a leader of the FEU as he claimed to *National Review Online*[92] he certainly would have been provided a uniform, and would remember it. In front of this room full of Tea Party members Rafael Cruz looked like a deer in the headlights when he was asked a question related to the actual Cuban Revolution. You can

---

[91] https://www.youtube.com/watch?v=P7_5P9kfMIM
[92] Exile and the Revolution, 11-4-11 Mario Loyola

see in the videos he does not have his usual commanding
delivery; he seems to be making it up as he goes along.
He is also embellishing his involvement or as my WWII
veteran Dad used to say, 'he's polishing his buttons'.
After being murdered in cold blood by the police on July
30, 1957, Frank Pais was buried in his M 26-7uniform
which outraged the Batista government.

Cuban Commentary *All the members of Frank Pais'
group wore uniforms at Santiago de Cuba. We were very
proud of those young people. Alfonso, age 83 (Translated
and edited for clarity)*

Chapter 39

Lie # 39

"They were rounding up people (in Santiago) and shooting them. It was a miracle of God I survived."[93]

Rafael Cruz makes another claim of a miraculous save by God, but one that he never mentioned until he was questioned about knowing Frank Pais. After being questioned about Frank Pais at the Weatherford Tea Party meeting, Rafael Cruz would tell an interviewer for Glenn Beck's *The Blaze*, Tara Setmayer that he escaped death twice, but there is no record of him mentioning two near death experiences at any other time.

Had this author not questioned Rafael Cruz about Frank Pais at the Weatherford, Texas Tea Party meeting, Rafael Cruz likely never would have fabricated or told this story. But why would he not want to burnish his credentials as a revolutionary by continuing to claim he escaped death twice?

In an article in the *National Review Online* Mario Loyola a fellow Cuban-American reports that by the age of 17[94], *'the young Rafael Cruz was already a leading*

[93] https://www.youtube.com/watch?v=oA_IAJEAxKs
[94] Exile and the Revolution, 11-4-11 Mario Loyola

FEU figure in Santiago de Cuba, the capital of Oriente, and a leader of its militant cell in that city. " This is truly stupendous, as Santiago de Cuba is 830 kilometers from Rafael Cruz's home in Matanzas. And how did Rafael Cruz manage to retain his straight A's while living and fighting 830 kilometers from home? Would anyone really believe that the Batista forces would have released a leader of FEU and not execute him?

Batista's police, under the direction of Interior Minister Rafael Diaz Balart had free reign to inflict whatever pain they could on Castro supporters. If they shot a young person in the head and killed them they would hang their body from a lamppost as a warning to others to avoid involvement in the Revolution.

If they assassinated a married man, they would go to his home and rape his wife, then plunder the home for any valuables. And Rafael Cruz wants people to believe that God saved him not once but twice, because God had other plans for him.

Within five years Rafael Cruz would have two daughters in the United States. He would abandon them and their mother and run off to Canada with another woman. He and that woman would have a son born in Calgary and when the boy was three years old Rafael

Cruz would abandon him and his mother in Canada and return to Texas.

If God really did save Rafael Bienvenido Cruz Diaz twice from death during the Cuban Revolution, couldn't God have had a better plan for Rafael Cruz' life?

Cuban Commentary: *Miracle of God or stupid lie? – Raul, age 43 (Translated and edited for clarity)*

Chapter 40

Lie #40

"I made my way back to my hometown of Matanzas and was arrested, held for several days in military detention, and was tortured then released."[95] *[This was in either June or July 1957 according to the National Review Online article*[96]*]*

He remembers the exact date and time of day that Fidel Castro's boat was to arrive from Mexico, November 30, 1956 at 7:00 am. He remembers the date he claims he received his student visa from the US government August 9, 1957. But he doesn't remember which month he was arrested and tortured and miraculously released? Let's give Rafael Cruz the unwarranted benefit of the doubt and say he was released from torture in June (the earlier of the two months) after which he decided to go to school in the US. Beginning in June he had to obtain a Cuban passport, research schools in the United States, find someone with perfect English skills to write his letters seeking admission, mail those letters by slow boat to the United States, and pray for a reply and acceptance before

---

[95] https://www.youtube.com/watch?v=m4PacOOaaHU

[96] Exile and the Revolution, 11-4-11 Mario Loyola

August 1. All while not raising the suspicions of the two government agents he claimed were following him 24/7.

Cuban Commentary: *He would have been tortured and killed in one session Pablo, age 64 (Translated and edited for clarity)*

Chapter 41

Lie #41a

From the mouth of a pastor, mind of a pig, Part 1

"Two years ago I met an engineer at a conference in Mexico who had been to Cuba recently. He told me girls 12 and 13 years old would be outside his hotel at the end of his day. And the girls would say, "Sir, for a plate of food I will go to bed with you."[97]

This is a disgusting lie from an evil man. I have been to Cuba 12 times. The first time I stayed in a hotel and every trip since I have stayed in casa particulars – bed and breakfasts. But I am always on the move; I see police officers walking beats throughout Havana, I know that all hotels have security people in their lobbies. I have never ever seen young girls prostituting themselves on sidewalks for food. Cubans are not starving. They may have limits on availability of meat, poultry, and fish but they have rice and beans aplenty.

More importantly, in visits to 96 parishes I have met many families with young daughters. I always bring along trinkets, chewing gum, candy, ball point pens, tea candles, and other items. Boys and girls thank me

---

[97] https://www.youtube.com/watch?v=kOTFYzM8pU0

profusely; many see me as a 'rich' American; but not one of them has ever offered me sex for food, money, or anything.

Rafael Cruz is revolting and in this author's mind, perverted. Why did it have to be 12 and 13 year old girls in his lie? Why could it not be teen girls or underage girls? Was he looking for maximum shock value, or perhaps articulating a personal fantasy? And this man Rafael Cruz has granddaughters ages six and four?

Cuban Commentary: *It would not be a surprise to me if this pig of a man ever had sex with young girls; after all where would he create such a lie if not from his own experience? He is not only a liar but a verbal pimp. – Yohandra, age 33 (Translated and edited for clarity)*

Lie #41b

From the mouth of a pastor, mind of a pig, Part 2

"A year later I was in Miami and I met a professor who had just returned from Cuba and I told him that story. He said, 'Oh casual prostitution is worse than that'. You have the housewives who shack up with tourists on the weekend." [98]

---

[98] Ibid

Sex with housewives is worse than sex with 12 year old girls? What kind of a vile and filthy man would make up such stories?

I have met many working mothers during my parish visits. They are moral and respectable; they clean their house on Saturday, go to church on Sunday morning, and spend Sunday afternoon with their family. They are not shacking up with tourists as this vile minded man Rafael Cruz would have his audiences believe. "Shacking up." Nice talk from a pastor.

Cuban Commentary: *He says degrading things about the wonderful women and mothers of Cuba. I would like to encounter him with my machete- Raul, age 43 (Translated and edited for clarity)*

Chapter 42

Lie # 42

"I came to this country not knowing the language, I worked full time went to school full time then opened my own company within 6 years. And I became a multimillionaire. If I can do it anybody can do it."[99]

From one side of his mouth Rafael Cruz boasts about being a multi-millionaire in other videos he laments being bankrupt and broke when Ted left for Princeton. He tells a tale about a preacher who was instructed by God to buy Rafael shoes because he had big holes in his and was using cardboard to keep his stocking feet from touching the ground. On what did he squander his multiple millions? He didn't even keep $100 to buy a pair of shoes?

But like every Cruz lie, his it seems to contradict other lies or undercut itself. He graduated from the University of Texas in 1961 with a degree in Mathematics. In the summer of 1962 he was a graduate student at UT.

So then he would have had his own company approximately 1968 in Austin, Texas. But then he claims

---

[99] https://www.youtube.com/watch?v=wqu9xAR4NKc

that a company in Canada had a 'big find' and hired him to be its vice president. That was where Ted was born, in Calgary. But it begs the question, why would someone who had his own company and was a multi-millionaire living the American dream toss it all aside to relocate to the frozen tundra of Calgary, Canada to become an employee? It is also interesting to note that Rafael Cruz never mentions the name of his company. Most people having built up a company and become a multi-millionaire would certainly be proud enough to name the company.

Perhaps there is some dark history in Rafael Cruz and Eleanor Wilson's past that drove them to leave the country?

Chapter 43

Lie #43

"I paid my way through school at $.50 an hour. When someone says to me I can't go to college because my family can't afford it, I tell them, "Go to work!"[100]

Since Rafael Cruz was violating federal labor laws by allegedly working for half the minimum wage with no work permit as a foreign national on a student visa, is he encouraging others to break the law?

---

[100] https://www.youtube.com/watch?v=xgwyK_NJL7U

Chapter 44

Lie # 44

"When Ted was ready to go to Princeton, my company
had gone bankrupt. I told him I could not afford to pay
his tuition; Ted said that's okay I'll get two jobs and pay
my own way."[101]

I suppose it's possible that at age 18 Ted Cruz
went out and got two part time jobs that netted him
$40,000 a year to pay tuition, fees, and books at
Princeton. Where did he work? While it's possible, it's
probably improbable since he was dealing with his Ivy
League classes, membership on the Princeton Debate
Team, and no doubt some type of social life.

Didn't Raffy Cruz (as Ted was known at
Princeton) qualify for any kind of financial aid, especially
as a Hispanic? Most financial aid is based on parental
income. Rafael Cruz had bankrupted his company during
his ongoing pursuit of the American dream; apparently he
believed that politics – the Reagan Campaign - were more
important than hard work.

Ted told the audience at his Liberty University
presidential campaign kick-off this story of getting two

---

[101] https://www.youtube.com/watch?v=aeMoKm1QZq0

jobs as well as sharing the fact that he had taken $100,000 in student loans. He also claimed he had recently paid off those student loans. So as in many Cruz family lies, the father and son tell varied versions.

Chapter 45

Lie # 45

"One thing you can count on Ted Cruz, he will tell you the truth."[102]

Rafael Cruz made this statement at Southern Conference where he was stumping for Ted Cruz's presidential campaign. Ted's lies begin in next chapter, 46. He embellishes Rafael's lies. The apple doesn't fall far from the tree, and it grows while on the ground.

---

[102] https://www.youtube.com/watch?v=zlLTjMYkmpY

Chapter 46

Lie # 46

In his speech at Liberty University kicking off his presidential campaign, Ted Cruz lied to 10,000 Christian college students when he referred to his father as *"A tall kid; jet black hair and skinny as a rail when he was involved in the Revolution."*[103]

Ted Cruz is as shameless as his father Rafael. To appear at what is touted in their TV advertising as the 'largest Christian university in the world' and tell a lie to 10,000 impressionable students is unconscionable. Viewing the photo from Ted's Senate Campaign ad (page 185, photo #2) does this young man look skinny as a rail? Photo #1 which was given by the Cruz Family to the Christian Broadcasting Network is a fake. It is someone's mug shot from somewhere, but not of Rafael Cruz nor from Cuba. This may seem like a petty issue but it's not; it's a lie fabricated to reinforce a fraud perpetrated on the Christian Broadcasting Network's David Brody. View the 2012 Cruz for Senate campaign ad,[104]

---

[103] https://www.youtube.com/watch?v=k-rRtJ5ypDo
[104] https://www.youtube.com/watch?v=O0ePwy6Q0UM

Chapter 47

Lie #47

"He was tortured and had his teeth kicked in, to this day his front teeth are not his own."[105] – Ted Cruz

It is very curious that Rafael Cruz has never mentioned this fact – that his own teeth were kicked out. Ted Cruz does and he has a habit of enhancing his father's lies (bombing buildings, throwing Molotov cocktails). Did Ted fabricate this tooth fairy tale for his speech at Hillsdale's Commencement where he contradicted his father as to how much money was in Rafael Cruz's underwear in August 1957? If Rafael really had his teeth kicked out of his mouth while being tortured, why did his father drive him home from his torture cell? Why did he not take him to a hospital or dentist?

"To this day his front teeth are not his own." What kind of statement is that? Once you lose any body part, it is never your own again.

---

[105] https://www.youtube.com/watch?v=3U-uOTJaSq0

Chapter 48

Lie #48

"He got a job paying 50 cents an hour, paid his way through school, graduated, and then went on to work toward the American Dream."[106]- Ted Cruz

Went on to work toward The American Dream? He got a girl pregnant in college. Less than a year after the birth of his first daughter they had a second daughter. He left his wife and two daughters and connected with Eleanor. They fled to Canada together. Ted said in his speech at Liberty University that his parents were both heavy drinkers, living fast lives.

Ted was born in 1970. He claims that in 1973 Rafael abandoned his second wife Eleanor and his son Ted and returned to Texas. American Dream?

---

[106] https://www.youtube.com/watch?v=MadsjArxcFM

Chapter 49

Lie #49

"He worked for fifty cents an hour. Now imagine if the minimum wage had been $2.00 an hour instead of being able to work for fifty cents. He might not have gotten that job, paid his way through school, and worked toward the American dream."[107] - Ted Cruz

In 1957 the US Minimum wage was set by law as $1.00 an hour. Rafael Cruz worked illegally and likely stole a job from a hard working American.

That is of course if he really did work as a dishwasher. Is he just romanticizing the most famous Cuban American dishwasher, Tony 'Scarface' Montana? Could he have just been a well-off Cuban foreign student who was supported by his parents back home?

---

[107] https://www.youtube.com/watch?v=dTw7JDB_E4E

Chapter 50

Lie #50

"Today he's a pastor in Dallas."[108] – Ted Cruz

Pastor: noun; a member of the clergy who leads a Congregation – Merriam Webster

This is quite odd, because even Rafael Cruz has never introduced himself as a pastor, minister, or any sort of religious occupation. If he is a pastor, where did he attend Seminary or Theology School? A pastor is defined as someone who leads a congregation. Where is Rafael Cruz's congregation? In every speech, Rafael Cruz talks about how the signers of the Declaration of Independence were pastors. Perhaps Ted Cruz is trying to elevate his father to the level of signers of the Declaration of Independence? Could the 'pastor' title just be a tax avoidance scam?

---

[108] https://www.youtube.com/watch?v=S_hlniN9jEM

Chapter 51

Lie #51

"My aunt, my father's kid sister returned to Cuba to visit some extended family. She herself had been imprisoned and tortured by Castro."[109] - Ted Cruz Cuba Democracy PAC, Miami

This again appears to be a Ted Cruz fabrication. In all his speeches, Rafael Cruz has never mentioned any anecdotes about his sister, let alone claim she was tortured. As much as Rafael hates Fidel Castro it is stunning that he never mentioned Castro torturing his sister. Why would his tortured aunt return to the scene of the crime?

Cuban Commentary: *Anyone who was tortured by Castro would never have returned. They could have been recaptured and sent to prison. -Elgis, age 62 (Translated and edited for clarity)*

---

[109] https://www.youtube.com/watch?v=IUXL3AD8m-w

Chapter 52

Lie #52

"Aunt Sonia visited Cuba and she ran into a childhood friend. He took her home, closed windows, drew drapes, and congratulated her for leaving. Then he wept for ten minutes. He felt bad not having escaped like she did."[110]
Ted Cruz Cuba Democracy PAC, Miami

Aunt Sonia is the only person in the past 58 years who allegedly was tortured and eventually returned to Cuba. One would think she would be fearful of being recaptured. I've had many conversations with people in Cuba in their homes. We've talked politics; I've poked fun at the Cuban system and the windows, drapes, and shutters were always open. Ted Cruz's appetite for fabricating and embellishing his father's tall tales knows no bounds.

Ted Cruz was making this speech before the Cuba Democracy PAC in Miami. Cuba Democracy PAC is one of the outfits in Miami populated by money grubbing parasites. In this case Mauricio Claver Carone who makes the Cruz men look like amateurs when it comes to fabricating stories.

---

[110] https://www.youtube.com/watch?v=pRPZXA4Qbgc

Cuban Commentary: *Dios Mio. El stupido! – Yaneli, age
46 (Translated and edited for clarity)*

Chapter 53

Lie #53

"He was a guerilla, throwing Molotov cocktails and blowing up buildings," Ted Cruz told the *Austin American-Statesman* for a profile published in January 2006. [111]

Ted later rescinded this in an interview with the *Dallas Morning News*. Several individuals who were actually involved in the Movement told me no buildings were blown up or firebombed except the police station in Santiago and a mill in Matanzas, Rafael Cruz's hometown. "Why would we destroy our country? We did not dislike property owners; we were fighting to get rid of Batista and his thugs."

The only bombing during the Revolution was at the Tinguaro Mill in Matanzas which was Rafael Cruz's hometown. The mill was bombed on May 27, 1957, shortly before Rafael Cruz claims he was arrested but more likely when he was home packing for his trip to the US and having a pocket sewn in his underwear.

---

[111] https://www.youtube.com/watch?v=MiAwihIcJuU

Cuban Commentary: *Bombs and bottles of flaming gasoline were not thrown about. Just at the police station on November 30, 1956. We valued our properties; we only despised Batista! – Ernesto, deceased 2014 age 86 (Translated and edited for clarity)*

Chapter 54

Lie # 54

"If not for the Transformative love of Jesus Christ I would have been raised by a single Mom."[112]- Ted Cruz, Presidential Campaign Kickoff Liberty University

This comment is unfair, self-serving, and implies that Ted, Rafael, and Eleanor were specially blessed somehow; the two daughters Rafael abandoned when he went off to Canada with Eleanor were left with a single Mom. Where was Jesus' Transformative love for them? They deserved to be loved by Jesus just as much as Ted. One of them had a long troubled life with drugs and bad men, and she died tragically of a drug overdose in 2011 according to Ted's book *A Time for Truth*.

If I had that kind of tragedy in my family's closet, I would not be crowing about having cornered the market on the transformative love of Jesus Christ in front of 10,000 Christian college students.

---

[112] https://www.youtube.com/watch?v=pQfox6C78bE

Chapter 55

Lie # 55
"I will tell you it is an incredible blessing to be the child of an immigrant who fled oppression and came here seeking freedom."[113]

Ted Cruz embellishes Rafael's lie about fleeing oppression. Rafael Cruz was a kid from a well-to-do family who went off to the US to attend university. This was common at the time among the Cuban elite families.

Marco Rubio used to tell that same lie throughout his political career but was exposed by Manuel Roig-Franzia, a Washington Post writer and author of 'The Rise of Marco Rubio'. His parents did not flee oppression either; they left Cuba in 1956.

Batistani Cuban-American politicians seem to have a difficult time telling the truth.

---

[113] https://www.youtube.com/watch?v=0lUiuS4_RGA

Chapter 56

Lie # 56

"And this teenage boy joined the Revolution. He joins that Revolution against Batista and he begins fighting with other teenagers to free Cuba from the dictator. This boy at age 17 finds himself in prison. Finds himself tortured and beaten and then at age 18 he flees Cuba." [114]
- Presidential Campaign Kickoff

In his own words, Rafael Cruz says in 1957 he was arrested, beaten, and tortured over a matter of a few days. And then he was miraculously released, the lady from the underground came and told him to leave the country which he did within two months. So how come Ted puts his imprisonment back to 1956, and then his departure to the University of Texas as 1957? And why does he tell this lie to 10,000 Christian university students? Why can't master liar Rafael Cruz and his lying protégé Ted Cruz get their lies in sync?

Cuban Commentary *These people are quite a thing to behold. If they were not so dangerous they would be*

---

[114] https://www.youtube.com/watch?v=AGvfpkFJ8xs

comical. – Yohandra, age 33 *(Translated and edited for clarity)*

Chapter 57

Lie #57

"Listen to Solzhenitsyn and the others who were in the gulags. They would pass notes to each other or whispered, "Did you hear what President Reagan said? What Jeanne Kirkpatrick said?"[115] Ted Cruz

Solzhenitsyn was exiled from the Soviet Union in 1974 and he came to the United States and settled in Vermont. This was six years before Ronald Reagan was elected president. Ted Cruz being Ted Cruz – this spinner of tall tales just can't seem to help himself. It begs the question: since Gulags did not have cable TV and these prisoners were in solitary confinement, how would they have heard President Reagan?

---

[115] https://www.youtube.com/watch?v=k-NrBnAqAm8

Chapter 58

Lie # 58

"In the 1960's there was a big discovery in Canada so a company hired me as vice president in Calgary, Canada." [116]

Rafael Cruz has various versions of the tale of why he and Eleanor relocated to Calgary, Canada though the other videos were not able to be found. In another story he says that there was on oil bust in the US in the 1960's. If the US oil business went bust why not the same in Canada? Look at oil production in the 60's in the graph on the next page. US oil production in the 1960's was on the increase. If Texas was having problems why not go to Colorado or Pennsylvania? Canada's oil is primarily heavy tar sand oil. There is no record of any big discovery in the late 60's.

Calgary is awfully cold especially for a Cuban expatriate. It's possible that Rafael Cruz's goal was to flee the country with his paramour, leaving his first spouse and two daughters behind to avoid legal, divorce, or child support issues. Perhaps Eleanor Elizabeth Darragh Wilson Cruz had some skeletons to hide?

---

[116] https://www.youtube.com/watch?v=tJ6AGaTB8o4

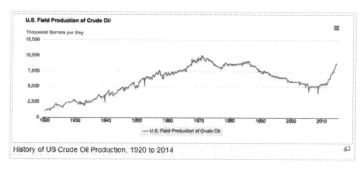

History of US Crude Oil Production, 1920 to 2014

Print quality may be bad

Chapter 59

Lie # 59 – 3 versions – one video[117]

Lie #59a

"We left Canada because there was a new prime minister elected in Canada at the end of 1974 who was a Socialist and there would be double taxation on the oil industry. I was lucky to be able to sell my company so we returned to US." – Rafael Cruz, The Blaze Interview, Tara Setmayer

Pierre Elliott Trudeau was the 15th Prime Minister of Canada from April 20, 1968 to June 4, 1979, and again from March 3, 1980 to June 30, 1984. There was no new prime minister coming along in late 1974. There is no documented history of double taxation of the oil industry. Who would want to buy a company if there was truly double taxation coming down the pike?

Lie #59b

Ted Cruz told Jeffrey Toobin of The New Yorker[118] that his parents separated and Rafael returned to Houston. He said that six months later Eleanor came home to Houston with Ted. There was no mention of Rafael going back to

---

[117] https://www.youtube.com/watch?v=JOk1GU6OEcc
[118] The Absolutist – June 30, 2014

get them. That version of the return by he and his mother was also included in articles in *Texas Monthly, Austin American Statesman and The Dallas Morning News*

How can you tell when a Cruz man is lying? He is lips are moving. We have read two totally different stories. One that contains multiple lies – new Socialist prime minister, double taxation of the oil industry, and selling his company. But wait; there is yet a third version.

I was watching it live streaming, Ted Cruz's campaign kick-off at Liberty University. As I watched him and heard his few 'white lies' about his father's past, I got frightened and said a silent prayer. "Dear God, hold his tongue. There are 10,000 Christian university students in that arena, young, ideological and probably naive. They can't be lied to; Ted, please don't lie to them!" Then Ted's free will overrode any prayers that I may have said. He didn't just tell a lie; he rolled out a whopper complete with histrionics.

Lie #59c

"When I was three my father decided to leave my mother and me. We were living in Calgary at the time he got on a plane and flew back to Texas. And he decided he didn't want to be married anymore and he didn't want to be a father to his three year old son.

And yet when he was in Houston a friend, a colleague from the oil and gas industry invited him to a Bible study. Invited him to Clay Road Baptist Church and there my father gave his life to Jesus Christ. And God transformed his heart.

And he drove to the airport, bought a plane ticket, and flew back to be with my mother and me. There are people who wonder if faith is real; I can tell you in my family there is not a second of doubt. " – Ted Cruz Presidential Campaign Kickoff, Liberty University March 25, 2015

It takes a lot of guts to go before 10,000 students at the largest Christian University in the world and tell a whopper of a lie. But give Ted Cruz credit; he knows how to play to a crowd - drinking too much, living a fast life, abandoning his family, and then "Joy, rapture! He gave his life to Jesus Christ." The likely truth is Lie #59b. Up to this point Rafael Cruz was going nowhere towards the American Dream.. Impregnated a girl twice during college; bounced from country to country for employment. He was living a fast life and was an alcoholic. Eleanor Darragh Wilson Cruz was obviously the brains in that household, having graduated from Rice University.

Chapter 60

Lie # 60

"Based on what I experienced in Cuba I became a student of Socialism. I remember when we had the last Socialist president, Jimmy Carter; double digit inflation, interest rates 20%, and the 82 (52) hostages taken in Iran. By the way it's no surprise that the hostages were released on Reagan's Inauguration Day. Iran knew he meant business. Well, I became a member of the Religious Roundtable, a group of pastors. We organized the largest gathering of evangelical ministers for Ronald Reagan at Reunion Arena in Dallas."[119]

What experience did Rafael Cruz have with Socialism in Cuba? He claims to have spent one month in the country in the past 56 years, though that is likely a lie. He was in Austin attending school, washing dishes, going to movies to learn to speak English, giving Rotary Club speeches, fathering two children, when would he have had time to keep up with Cuban politics ? He didn't even learn about the rich being evil and oppressing the poor, nor redistributing the wealth until he claims he went home for a month? No one shared that with him?

---

[119] https://www.youtube.com/watch?v=vashAEBa8aA

Can Rafael Cruz produce one photo of himself with Ronald Reagan if he had so much sway in the Reagan campaign? How about a photo of him and members of the Religious Roundtable? In 1974 he was an alcoholic that had abandoned his wife and son in Canada, after having abandoned a wife and two daughters in Texas. Five years later, 1979 he is a pastor and is among the elite pastors in the US?

Where had he attended Seminary? When was he ordained? As a pastor where was his Congregation? How was he supporting his family?

Chapter 61

Lie #61
"Cuba shipped weapons to North Korea one month before Obama made the announcement about resuming relations with Cuba in December, 2014.[120]

Complete lie. Cuba shipped 1958 era MiGs to North Korea to be repaired and it was in July 2013, 17 months before the agreement between Barak Obama and Raul Castro was announced.

---

[120] https://www.youtube.com/watch?v=wANgbKBL3x0

Chapter 62

Lie #62

"The Castro government would tell children in school, if you hear your parents talking against the government it is your civic responsibility to turn them in." [121]

This statement, on old Cold War fable is so incredibly ridiculous.

Cuban Commentary: *I always hear how the American people are so intelligent. How can it be possible that they believe this man, this gusano? (worm) – Jose, age 68 (Translated and edited for clarity)*

---

[121] https://www.youtube.com/watch?v=LWqN-WAqdVs

Chapter 63

Lie #63

"What's my opinion of the Obama Castro deal? For years the USSR was propping up the Cuban Regime. When the USSR collapsed then Chavez in Venezuela picked up the tab. Well right now, oil has dropped to less than half, Venezuela is having real economic problems, so now it was an unprecedented time when the Cuban regime was shaky. There was a possibility it might even crumble and here comes Comrade Obama handing out a lifeline to Cuba. And propping up that regime that was teetering." (2014)[122]

I have been along the coast of Cuba and seen container ships arriving daily from China with consumer goods. The lunacy of pressing the embargo is driven by a handful of morally corrupt Batistani Cuban-Americans in Congress – Marco Rubio, Mario Diaz Balart, and Ileana Ros Lehtinen and now Ted Cruz. They wish to continue to inflict pain on the Cuban people as retaliation for not rising up against Castro; this conduct is criminal, amoral, and un-Christian.

---

[122] https://www.youtube.com/watch?v=7I2raOWnJqs

I have long considered it good fortune that Osama Bin Laden and his family's millions never came calling on Fidel Castro. That could have been devastating to our country. Engagement is the answer.

Chapter 64

Lie #64

"In 1963 the Supreme Court took the bible and prayer out of school. What happened? The teen pregnancy rate skyrocketed."[123]

Quoting Rafael Cruz, "Marxists say whatever they have to that furthers their cause." No, teen pregnancy rates did not skyrocket; the teen birth rate actually dropped from the 1960's to the 1980's. Is Rafael Cruz a closet Marxist?

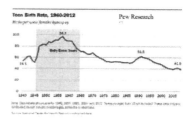

---

[123] https://www.youtube.com/watch?v=ieb1SnwOiGk

Chapter 65

Lie #65

*"I've met so many Christians that tell me Evolution is a
scientific fact. Baloney! I am a scientist; there is nothing
scientific about Evolution."*[124]

He has a Degree in Mathematics from University
of Texas, 1961. What is the biggest of the lies contained
in the quote above? *"I am a scientist."*

---

[124] https://www.youtube.com/watch?v=gZWG-I4IINQ

Chapter 66

Lie #66a

"When he was growing up I used to tell Ted when I lost my freedom in Cuba I was able to come here. If we lose our freedoms here, where will we go?"[125]

When did he lose his freedom in Cuba? His parents were earning 13 times the national median family income. He opted to leave of his own will in 1957 like many youth of privilege to attend an American University, two years before the success of Castro's Revolution.

What kind of a bizarre thing is that to tell to an eight year old? Scare the child and scar him for life. Does anyone besides this bizarre old man believe that we could lose our freedoms in the United States? Perhaps Rafael Cruz had a premonition that 30 years hence a black man would be elected president and that made his skin crawl, and not just any black man but a Socialist-Marxist.

Lie #66b

"I lost my freedom once; I am not willing to lose it again. I will die fighting for it."[126]

---

[125] https://www.youtube.com/watch?v=8qHuEUR7D7U
[126] Ibid

Rafael Cruz builds on his original lie and seeks to incite Tea Party members against the Obama Administration. He continually projects hatred for Obama. Perhaps he inherited the racism that likely got his mother dismissed from her teaching job.

Cuban Commentary: When did the boy of privilege lose his freedom? He probably lost it when he impregnated a girl in university. – Luis Enrique, age 26 (Translated and edited for clarity)

Chapter 67

Lie #67

"When the righteous are in authority the people rejoice. When the wicked are in authority the people mourn. If the righteous are not voting, if the righteous are not running for office, what have you got left? The wicked electing the wicked. That's what's happening in America and it is our fault. We need to get people of faith to vote and vote Biblical values."[127]

This is pure regurgitated blather from the Evangelical Right. Writing this book and conducting the research including viewing hours and hours of video of Rafael Cruz has left me scared for America. Not scared of the 'Socialist/Marxist/communist Obama-Hillary Clinton 'ma-cheen'.

Rafael Cruz is stealthily waging his own jihad on behalf of his son Ted against the political establishment and seeks to implement his own version of Sharia law. 'Enough of being politically correct; it's time to be Biblically correct. Our laws should be based on Biblical principles. It is time to return the Bible as the only textbook in American schools, as it was at the time of our

---

[127] https://www.youtube.com/watch?v=UsNO-kqBqSg

Founding Fathers.' This is truly frightening. Substitute a word here or there and Rafael Cruz could be an Islamic mullah.

Chapter 68

Lie #68

"At least half the judges in the Supreme Court are over 80 years old." [128]

Antonin Scalia, 79; Anthony Kennedy 78; Clarence Thomas 66; Ruth Bader Ginsburg, 82; Stephen Breyer, 76; John Roberts, 60; Samuel Alito, 65, Sonia Sotomayor, 60; Elena Kagan, 55

This was one of a plethora of lies Rafael Cruz spewed at the Denton County (TX) Lincoln Reagan Dinner in 2014, all of which drew applause.

What else would you expect from a world class pathological liar hell bent on getting his son elected President of the United States? It appears that Rafael Cruz's math skills are as poor as his honesty.

Cruz was introduced by Texas State Senator Jane Nelson, a woman I have admired for many years and a woman of integrity. She asked Rafael to tell how he raised a US Senator. He droned on about force feeding Ted books on right wing theory and economics. Had Senator Nelson known his record of fathering and

---

[128] https://www.youtube.com/watch?v=EJRO3iAKuUE

bandoning children, one has to wonder if she would not
have stood beside Rafael Cruz let alone introduce him.

Chapter 69

Lie #69

"Before Castro Cuba was a very wealthy country. It had one of the strongest economies in the world. 8th highest economy in the world and the highest economy in Latin America."[129]

Denmark had the 8th highest economy in the world in 1955 and Venezuela had the highest in Latin America at #4. Cuba was not even ranked in the Top 100 worldwide. The United States at #1 had a per capita income of $5,680. Cuba's per capita income was $400 per year in 1955. [130]

Another lie by Rafael Cruz designed to make people fear that President Obama (Castro II in Rafael's world) will destroy the US economy

---

[129] https://www.youtube.com/watch?v=HvgMKssF0EA
[130] nationmaster.com – data presented in Lie #69 Video

Chapter 70

Lie #70

"Cuba had a top medical system and Castro destroyed it"[131]

At the time of the revolution Cuba's infant mortality rate exceeded 60 deaths per 1,000 live births. Twelve mothers died during delivery for every 10,000 births. There were 6,000 doctors in the entire country, almost all of whom were concentrated in the capital of Havana. Life expectancy was below 60 years of age. Public health services were nonexistent in the countryside, where more than half the population lived. Since that time Cuba's health care system, which is 100 percent government owned, has developed into a pinnacle of achievement in Socialist medicine.

Article 50 of Cuba's Constitution guarantees the right to health protection and care. The constitution provides for free medical and hospital care through a system of rural medical service networks, polyclinics, hospitals, and treatment centers for preventative and specialized medicine. Free dental care, health education,

---

regular medical examinations and general vaccinations are also guaranteed.

Cuba's infant mortality rate has been reduced in 2013 by more than 90 percent, to just 4.76 deaths per 1,000 live births. Compare that to the US rate of 5.2 deaths per 1000 live births.[132] The maternal mortality rate has dropped to just over four deaths per 10,000 births.

The decline in delivery-related deaths can be attributed to the fact that 100 percent of Cuban births are attended by skilled health workers. When a mother goes home with her baby a pediatrician and nurse visit the home every week for one month. Then the nurse continues on for five more months.

Today Cuba boasts more than 66,000 physicians and is able to send thousands of its own doctors to provide medical care to the world's poor and oppressed. In 2014 Cuba has 30,000 medical personnel on missions in 103 countries.

Researchers in Cuba have developed a Lung Cancer Vaccine CimaVax which is now being brought to the United States for clinical trials.

In 2005 after Hurricane Katrina Fidel Castro reached out and offered to send medical personnel to

---

[132] CIA World Factbook

New Orleans. President George W. Bush's press secretary gave a response that was akin to a verbal middle finger. Rafael Cruz's reason for lying about Cuba's medical system? Rafael Cruz's goal here is to make people believe that national healthcare like Obamacare destroys medical care.

Cuban Commentary: *My God, we have one of the best medical systems in the world. We have excellent doctors and treatment and we pay nothing. – Yaneli, age 46 (Translated and edited for clarity)*

Author's Note: *In 2012 I was diagnosed with Early Onset Alzheimer's. I was told there was no cure, just pharmaceuticals to 'manage' the illness. Several months later I developed one of the rare symptoms of EO AZ, a severe stutter.*

At that point I had to walk away from my career as a sales trainer and made it known to my circle of friends what my situation was. Doctor friends in Cuba emailed and insisted that I come to a clinic in Cuba, CIREN. Translated the acronym stands for International Center for Neurological Restoration.

It is renowned for treatment of Parkinson's, Alzheimer's, and head and spinal injuries. Patients come from around the world. I became the first American ever admitted as a patient and was there for five weeks. The unique treatments did not cure me, but they eliminated my stutter and improved my fluency scores and overall sense of well-being. When I returned home my neuropsychologist was stunned. - PL

(My CIREN before and after video included in Lie #70 video)

Memo to Rafael Cruz: Article 50 of Cuba's Constitution guarantees the right to health protection and care for all Cuban citizens. Why not renounce your US citizenship – face it your son Raffy will never be president – and reclaim your Cuban citizenship and travel to your mother country for world class medical care? Then you won't have to worry about your friend Sarah Palin's dreaded death panels. Of course you may have to answer questions about William Soler's mysterious death in 1957, your big year when you headed to the land of the free and the home of the brave thanks to the Batista Regime and the 'four year student visa' you convinced them to let you leave Cuba on.

Chapter 71

Lie #71

"Obama and his crowd don't care at all about homosexuals or homosexual marriage. They just want to destroy the traditional family so that people will worship government as their God."[133]

How does one even formulate a response to this bizarre claim? But one can opine that with his personal track record of marriage, divorce, and spousal and child abandonment, Rafael Cruz has done more damage to traditional families than President Obama ever could.

---

[133] https://www.youtube.com/watch?v=dtm-fY6w2BQ

Chapter 72

Lie # 72

"My company was bankrupt and my shoes had holes in the bottoms, both of them. I was putting cardboard in them to keep my feet dry. Pastor John bought me some shoes."[134]

Rafael Cruz often trashes the 'handout generation' people who are always expecting things to be given to them, especially by the government. He says what they need is to get a job. Why didn't Rafael Cruz get a job instead of taking handouts? He could have even gone back to his early career expertise, washing dishes.

Why not shop at Salvation Army? Where was his money going? Drinking? Womanizing? The Reagan Campaign?

And didn't he boast in an earlier video that he became a multi-millionaire? When his company started going south, why didn't he stash some cash aside? He didn't even set aside $100 to buy a new pair of shoes?

---

[134] https://www.youtube.com/watch?v=nXVov6YalqA

Chapter 73

Lie # 73

"Blacks need to be educated. Margaret Sanger was the
founder of Planned Parenthood. It was founded to control
the Black population. Do you know that most abortion
clinics are in Black neighborhoods? Blacks should be
outraged. Do you know it was Republicans who gave
Blacks Civil Rights? Did you know that the Ku Klux Klan
was made up of all Democrats from the South?
Before the minimum wage was instilled in 1938 Black
unemployment and White unemployment were the same –
With the minimum wage Black unemployment rose to
25%. If we raise the minimum wage Black unemployment
will go up, but the average Black doesn't understand that.
Blacks should all be Republicans."[135]

According to Thomas Sowell, African-American
economist, social theorist, political philosopher, and
author, *'by1942 the black unemployment rate was down*
to 4.7% (US Census) and in the late 1940s, the
unemployment rate among young black men was not only
far lower than it is today (2005) but was not very
different from unemployment rates among young whites

---

[135] https://www.youtube.com/watch?v=NFk1lPyInao

the same ages. Every census from 1890 through 1930 showed labor force participation rates for blacks to be as high as, or higher than, labor force participation rates among whites. [136]

Rafael Cruz implies that an 'average black' - whatever that is, happens to be an ignorant person. Is Rafael Cruz making the case that the minimum wage should be eliminated so blacks can be hired at rock bottom wages? In what way does Rafael Cruz define an 'average black?' I have many African-American friends who are intelligent, articulate, well-educated individuals, far more so than a Cuban cracker like Rafael Cruz.

It is little wonder Rafael Cruz's audiences are lily white. This is probably some lingering Cuban racism which caused his mother to relinquish her teaching job. I am not even going to dignify Rafael Cruz's other racist statements with a comment.

---

[136] Thomas Sowell, Real Clear Politics 11-15-05

Chapter 74

Lie # 74

"In Cuba today, food is rationed. As a matter of fact meat is limited to ½ pound per person per month. That's what Socialism does to people."[137]

Rafael Cruz has not set foot on Cuban soil since 1957, when as the son of an affluent Cuban family he headed off to the United States and the University of Texas. Yet people seem to think of him as a sage of all things Cuban. This is an outright, absolute lie but one that draws gasps, 'oh mercy me', and shaking heads in his audiences. And how much is a half a pound in Cuba, which is on the metric system? A good liar always covers the details; Rafael Cruz is a sloppy liar.

As much as he hates Barak and Michelle Obama (old Cuban racism dies hard) and is constantly comparing President Obama to 'that bearded dictator I left behind' this lie is just one of his many subliminal inferences this is what we will face in the United States if we don't thwart Obama and sidetrack Hillary Clinton.

---

[137] https://www.youtube.com/watch?v=ZZOeyhHISvM

Cuban Commentary: He claims that *our wives and 12 year old daughters are prostitutes, and we only get less than ½ of a kilo of meat per month. Perhaps this man Rafael Cruz's brain is rotted by syphilis. – Pablo, age 64 (Translated and edited for clarity)*

Chapter 75

Lie # 75

"The United States of America was formed to honor the word of God. If you hear Obama recite the Pledge he always skips under God from Pledge of Allegiance. "[138]

Four times President Obama is shown on video reciting the Pledge of Allegiance with 'Under God'. And 'Under God' was added to the Pledge in 1954.

It is somewhat ironic that the Pledge of Allegiance was written by Francis Bellamy, a Christian Socialist minister and published in the Youth's Companion on September 8, 1892. Initially, the pledge was begun with the right hand over the heart, and after reciting "to the Flag," the arm was extended toward the Flag, palm-down. In World War II, the salute too much resembled the Nazi salute, so it was changed to keep the right hand over the heart throughout.

Socialism, Nazism, there are enough 'isms' in the Pledge's history to make Rafael Cruz's head explode.

---

[138] https://www.youtube.com/watch?v=eGSH-n8AOXw

Chapter 76

Lie #76

"Obama is a Marxist, another Fidel Castro. President Obama wants to destroy god; he wants government to be your god. And truth to Marxists is whatever they say that advances their cause. I'd like to send Obama back to Chicago, Kenya, or Indonesia."[139]

This is certainly an example of that old expression, 'the pot calling the kettle black.' And by the explanation in the sentence of what truth is to Marxists, Rafael Cruz would qualify as a Marxist, just like his old Hope and Change savior of the country, that bearded dictator he left behind, Fidel Castro.

Cuban Commentary – *they need to send Rafael Cruz back to Cuba to be interrogated about the murders of William Soler and the other three boys. Yohandra, age 33 (lawyer) (Translated and edited for clarity)*
You shall not bear false witness against your neighbor. – Exodus 20:16

---

[139] https://www.youtube.com/watch?v=Cbra2pwUPvE

Chapter 77

God Speaks to Rafael Cruz

"In my quiet time with the Lord, what I heard from the Lord was – the pastors are key to turning this country around Mandate I received from the Lord was, go tell my pastors to go warn my people [to vote for righteous people or the country will be gone]"[140]

Rafael Cruz claims he has done 29 pastors conferences this year and has at least 15 more before the end of the year. His main shtick is that most of the signers of the Declaration of Independence were pastors and that the 17 grievances in the Declaration of Independence were first preached from the pulpits.

Hence he claims that he has been chosen by God to reawaken the political fervor in pastors and get them to campaign for the GOP nominee (presumably his son Ted Cruz) in 2016. He urges them to have a voter registration table in each church in America and to pass out voter guides and to not worry about the IRS threatening to revoke their 501(c)3 status.

"Go tell my pastors to go warn my people?" I would think God Almighty would have a more important

---

[140] https://www.youtube.com/watch?v=IFAtTTFtIUg

message for Rafael Cruz: "Stop lying, and stop misrepresenting yourself as a pastor." Or perhaps like George Burns as God had John Denver tell that pompous televangelist in the movie *Oh God*, "Go sell shoes."

Chapter 78

Pledging to Rafael Cruz

At the end of each speech, Rafael Cruz has his audience stand and face one another or face him, raise their right hands and repeat this pledge after him.

"We will make a covenant to one another in a loud voice before God:

"With a firm reliance on the protection of divine providence, we mutually pledge to each other our lives, our fortunes, and our sacred honor.

To do all we can to restore righteousness to America, rule of law, free enterprise, and make America again a shining city on a hill for the Glory of God. "[141]

As an observer, it's quite hysterical. This circus-like act calls to mind Harvey Korman on the hilltop in the movie Blazing Saddles swearing in his posse. "I . . . I . . . Your name . . . Your name."

As a showman, PT Barnum had nothing on Rafael Cruz. Of course, Rafael Cruz seems to have as his core philosophy PT Barnum's most famous quote, "There's a sucker born every minute."

---

[141] https://www.youtube.com/watch?v=a02J5aTBscc

Chapter 79

Illegal Alien's View on Immigration

When asked what he thought of amnesty by *Blaze* correspondent Tara Setmayer, Rafael Cruz said, *"It is fundamentally wrong to reward people who have broken the law over and above people who have gone through the [immigration] process."*[142]

Rafael Cruz arrived on a student visa in violation of financial and language requirements, did not qualify for a Social Security card, and worked for one half of the minimum wage.(so he claims) And he criticizes those he deems to be here 'illegally'? Again, this is the pot calling the kettle black.

---

[142] https://www.youtube.com/watch?v=RdqD-R-kTv4

Chapter 80

Something's Wrong with This Picture

According to his words, Rafael Cruz's parents were affluent in 1950's Cuba. His father was a salesman for RCA and made $300 per month. His mother was a public school teacher; she made $140 per month. That gave them an annual household income of $5,280. The median annual household income in Cuba at the time was $400. The Cruz Diaz household income was 13 times the national median.

This begs the question, why was Rafael sent off with 'what few dollars his father could scrounge for bus fare to Austin and a few hamburgers along the way'. There is no data available from the University of Texas as to what tuition was from 1957 through 1961. However in 1970 – the earliest year that is recorded the tuition was $270 per semester for an out-of-state student[143] – exactly three weeks earnings for Mr. and Mrs. Rafael Bienvenido Cruz Diaz.

Why on earth did Rafael Bienvenido Cruz Diaz have to go pearl diving in a restaurant kitchen (old diner dishwasher joke) for $.50 an hour and risk being arrested

---

[143] UT Tuition chart, appendix

by the INS and deported back to Cuba for working in violation of federal law? Why couldn't his parents just pay his tuition and give him more free time to watch movies, give speeches at Rotary Clubs, and chase American girls?

The answer is that they likely did support him financially. There are too many lies built in to his hobo tale of arriving at UT penniless with just the clothes on his back and having the red carpet rolled out. How would he have managed as he claimed to travel back to Cuba in the summer of 1959 on his dishwasher wages?

And in 1961, the year he would graduate he got a young lady pregnant and they had a baby girl in November. The following year 1962 while he was in graduate school he got her pregnant again and this daughter was also born in November, 6 days before her older sister's birthday. This qualified them as 'Irish Twins' – siblings born within 365 days of one another.

How did Rafael Cruz support himself, his wife, and two infant daughters on his $.50 an hour dishwasher's wages? It is probably likely he was receiving money from his parents in Cuba. But a hero's tale of working for fifty cents an hour for four years and paying for school is a much more captivating tale for

Evangelical and Tea Party audiences, while omitting
details of alcoholism, child births, child abandonment,
and two abandoned spouses.

Chapter 81
Theory of What Really Happened

I'd like to offer a theory of what might have really happened. Rafael Cruz, bilingual son of affluent parents wanted to attend college in the US. He bought his exit visa from Batista on January 2, 1957 by targeting four youths as troublemakers, including William Soler who were tortured and murdered by Cuban Police. He flew by Eastern Airlines to Austin, Texas and entered the University of Texas. He did not work as a dishwasher.

Readers can compare the two photos that the Cruz men have presented as being Rafael Cruz at age 18. The mug shot with the #166 was given to the Christian Broadcasting Network to include in a video titled "From Dishwasher to the White House" produced in April 2015.[144] The photo of the bearded bespectacled man was part of Ted Cruz's Senate campaign ads in 2012 under the tagline 'he came from a family of fighters.' Comparing the photo of Ted with his parents Rafael and Eleanor in Calgary, it's easy to conclude that the mug shot photo is not Rafael Cruz but just another scam pulled off by the Cruz Cons. The Cruz family treats photos as though they

---

[144] This video has since been removed from CBN's website

vere taken on the Texas Giant at Six Flags. And how vould someone 'fleeing Cuba' get a copy of his alleged mug shot? What an insult to any intelligent person's ntellect by the Cruz Cons.

Photo #1 (top) mug shot given by Cruz to Christian Broadcasting Network – person unknown; #2 Photo from Cruz for Senate campaign of 'Rafael when he fled Cuba' (age 18) #3 Family in 1974 Cuban Commentary: *This photo (#1) is quite comical. No one taken captive by Diaz Balart's gamberros (thugs) would have lived as long as it would have taken to fabricate that collar with the number 166. – Alfonso, age 83 (Translated and edited for clarity)*

Chapter 82

Cuba's Museums of the Revolution

Cuba has two splendid Museums of the Revolution, one in Havana and one in Santiago de Cuba at the eastern end of the island. I have been to Santiago several times including Pope Benedict XVI's Mass on March 26, 2012. The museum in Santiago is in the former Moncada Barracks where Castro and his supporters made their first attack against Batista's Dictatorship on July 26, 1953. The museum in Havana is in a building which had been the Presidential Palace until the demise of Batista. Both museums have bullet holes preserved in their walls. I have visited both museums during Mission trips to Cuba.

There are many impressive exhibits, including hand typed rosters of the men and female nurses who participated in the major events of the Revolution. This includes the battle at Santiago de Cuba on November 30, 1956 when Castro and his men were supposed to arrive aboard the yacht Granma. This is the battle where Rafael Cruz claims that he was with Frank Pais and others when they engaged Batista's forces and police, and that he saw Pais 12 hours before he was killed. He also claims that God spared him from being shot in the head like all the other prisoners because God had plans for his life.

I have reviewed rosters at both museums, and have asked companions to also scan the rolls, and the name Rafael Bienvenido Cruz Diaz does not appear in any form on any of the rosters. It would certainly be expected that such a heroic character would be memorialized.

Chapter 83

Questions for Pastor Cruz

Pastor Cruz claims moral superiority to most men and he is a very public figure. Therefore he should answer these questions in a public forum.

Morality gut check for Pastor Cruz:

1. Did you attend seminary? What institution?
2. Did you attend theology school? What institution?
3. Do you have a degree in theology?
4. When and where were you ordained?
5. Into what denomination were you ordained?
6. Did you obtain your pastor's credentials from the internet?
7. At what church do you pastor?
8. What religion is your congregation?
9. You are introduced to groups as a professor of Bible and Theology; professors have doctorates. Where did you earn your doctorate in Bible and Theology?
10. What is your affiliation with Suzanne Hinn, wife of TV miracle healer Benny Hinn and Purifying Fires Ministries?
11. You are introduced to groups as Purifying Fires Ministries Director of Mexico and Central

America? Do you have any proof of any religious activities in any of those countries?

12. Does God talk to you as you claim in your speeches?

13. If so, what does God talk to you about?

14. Where and when did you get a degree as a scientist?

15. You never say a good thing about the people of Cuba. Do you hate Cuba and the Cuban people?

16. Do you share the hatred of the Cuban people that Rafael Diaz Balart and the other Batistanis in Miami have long had because the Cuban people never rose up against Fidel Castro?

17. Did you ever marry the woman you impregnated during your senior year at the University of Texas?

18. Your second daughter was born in Dallas. Did you live in Dallas?

19. Why was your second daughter born in Dallas? Had the mother left you?

20. Did you ever live in New Orleans?

21. Where did you and Eleanor meet?

22. What year did you and Eleanor move to Canada?

23. Had you divorced the mother of your two daughters before you moved to Canada?

24. Were you and Eleanor married when Ted was born?

25. Where and when were you and Eleanor married?

26. You filed for and were granted a divorce from Eleanor in Harris County in 1997. Is it appropriate for a pastor who preaches about family values and the sanctity of marriage to file for divorce from his wife?

Chapter 84

Thirty Day Language Wonder

I serve as an English as a Second Language (ESL) teacher for an organization called Literary Instruction for Texas (LIFT). I am very impressed by the students from around the globe who are immigrants and work jobs yet put time and effort into learning the English language. My grandparents who came here in 1906 and members of their generation spoke their native tongues until they went to the grave.

These ESL students work diligently to learn one of the two hardest languages in the world, the other being Chinese. These immigrant students work jobs (legally), have families and household duties yet they devote two hours two nights a week to work at learning the English language. (Plus homework time)

On average it takes about two years for a person to learn progressively and become fluent in English. Some even take separate classes to help them minimize their accent.

Rafael Cruz claims to have taught himself the English language by sitting in a movie theater every night for thirty days. That was the recommendation he claims from an English teacher he had in Cuba. All that would do would be to make him a parrot. Listen to teens in other countries that do not speak English but can sing along with any English language Pop Music song – they parrot the singers.

Listen to Rafael Cruz speak in You Tube videos: (all phonetic SIC)

as a motter of fac	crees-chee-an
so-shee-alism	en-yee-neer
deeshwasher	deeshes
pash-io-net	pate-ree-ots
ay-you-cate	joung people
Aus-ting	Chee-ca-go
Tre-shur	Moss-ah-choosetts
Sole-gee-ers	

I boardered a ferry to Key West

my letter of asseptance from UT

cashual prostitution

press-ee-dent of the United States

Me-chell Obama

In no way am I generalizing or making fun of anyone with an accent. But Rafael Cruz claims to have learned to speak fluent English by watching movies for

0 consecutive days in 1957. And he has had fifty eight years of living in North America to perfect his dialect yet Rafael Cruz sounds like he just got off the boat.

Rafael Cruz's intent here is apparent: to besmirch today's immigrants and the 'Press 1 for Spanish' technology by implying 'if I did it in 30 days why can't they?' He seems to love to hate immigrants almost as much as he hates Fidel Castro and President Obama.

I would suspect that early in his high school years Rafael Cruz and his well to do family decided he would go to school in the US and engaged an English professor to teach him the language. He claims in a CBN video to host David Brody that his English language when he arrived in the US was limited to 'Tom is a boy Mary is a girl.'[145] How asinine; they certainly did not get their money's worth from that professor.

---

[145] http://www.cbn.com/tv/4208930061001

Chapter 85

Dominionist

I am not a Biblical Scholar. Come to think of it neither is Rafael Cruz probably – he's just good at throwing out verses like a carnival barker. I will leave it to those with greater knowledge and insight into Theology and the Bible to comment about his goal of turning the United States into a Dominionist Nation.

Dominionists – destined to be king or priest; be anointed to take dominion over the country; a political and religious philosophy that seeks to make the United States government a Christian theocracy. Rafael Cruz says Ted is destined to be a king. No doubt Rafael sees himself as a high priest.

Rafael Cruz didn't have dominion over his own life, his two families, his drinking, his bankrupt business, etc. How can he and Ted take Dominion over the United States?

To get an overview of Rafael Cruz's view of a Dominionist society where the church has influence over every aspect of society: the media, arts and entertainment, professional sports, education, business, government,

view the video titled Religious Fanaticism. [146] Rafael Bienvenido Cruz Diaz – he's angrier than Reverend Jeremiah Wright, more extreme that Ayatollah Khamenei.

---

[146] https://www.youtube.com/watch?v=YpUtt3F09A8

Chapter 86

Life Imitates Art Rafael Cruz's Story Board

Rafael Cruz probably sees himself as a cross between James Bond, Jason Bourne, and the Man from U.N.C.L.E. The inspiration for the Lady from the Underground who supposedly came to his house after he was supposedly released by the supposed colonel after he was supposedly beaten and tortured likely came from one of his favorite TV shows, *Hogan's Heroes.*

With all the places that his mother could have sewn the money pocket such as inside his pants or his shirt, where in the world did the underwear ruse come from? Could it be from the story of the Underwear Bomber who tried to take down a Delta Airlines flight in 2009?

And surely the inspiration for the dishwasher had to be Tony Montana from the movie *Scarface. 'Don't be callin' me no f***in' dishwasher or I'll kick your f***in' monkey ass.'* Al Pacino, formerly the most famous Cuban-American dishwasher, now has been upstaged by Rafael Cruz. After all, Rafael Cruz probably fancied

imself a tough guy having collected weapons and fought
n the revolution. *'Say hello to my leetle friend!'*

As far as the parent-child duo, curiously I see a
parallel between Rafael Cruz and Patsy Ramsay, as well
as Ted Cruz and Jon Benet Ramsay.

Both parents were controlling helicopter parents
before the term had been coined. They pushed their
children to fulfill their own dreams. Jon Benet was
pushed into competing in beauty pageants from a very
young age.

Rafael Cruz claims he started declaring the Word
of God to Ted at four years old and making declarations
over him. Rafael proclaimed that Ted had been gifted
above any man Rafael knew and God has destined Ted
Cruz for greatness.[147]

Ted Cruz was given a Biblical world view at age
8, was made to study books of economic theory and talk
Carter-Reagan politics every night at the dinner table. At
age 12 he joined a group of teens who had to memorize
the US Constitution as part of a group called the
Constitutional Collaborators. He had to go around to
Rotary Clubs and perform, giving presentations on the
Constitution. Perhaps that is where Rafael Cruz found the

---

[147] https://www.youtube.com/watch?v=YpUtt3F09A8

template for his lie about 'speaking to Rotary Clubs around Austin about Castro' when he could not speak English back in 1958.

Rafael Cruz probably harbored fantasies of returning to Cuba with Rafael Diaz Balart and the Miami Cartel to take control of the government. Since that seemed destined not to happen, he lied his son into politics.

Chapter 87

He was for Castro Before He was Against Him

(Apologies to Secretary of State John Kerry)

Why does Rafael Cruz have a Batistani-like visceral hatred of Fidel Castro? The Batistanis in South Florida go ballistic at the mention of Fidel Castro's name. They almost burned MLB Marlins Manager Ozzie Guillen at the stake for complimenting Fidel in an off the cuff comment. He was suspended for several games by the Marlins and was forced to make a cash contribution to one of the Cuban NGOs in the cesspool of corruption known as Miami. Rafael Cruz never lived under Fidel Castro. His tales claim that he 'fought on the side of Castro against Batista'.

And then at some point he began to despise Castro. He claims to have visited Cuba for one month less than five months after Castro took over, but that story is highly suspect since he piles so many lies into that story, about all the 'Socialist policies' he falsely claimed Castro had enacted. Nevertheless he doesn't claim to have been harassed, arrested, or tortured, nor had any property confiscated by the Castro government during that thirty day period.

So why after 56 years does he have such hatred for Fidel Castro? Could it be because he was in fact a full-fledged Batistani, like the Diaz Balarts, Rep. Ileana Ros Lehtinen and other thugs in the Miami Cartel? Could it be that the blowback to Marco Rubio over Rubio's lies about his parents' migration caused Rafael and Ted Cruz to collaborate and concoct a whopper of a story? *"Dad, most people only oppose one dictator. Let's tell them you opposed two. That way you will look like an amazing super hero."*

One last thought on this Castro hatred. Rafael Cruz's life has been nothing near the American Dream. Abandoned wives and children, alcoholism, bankrupt company, dubious credentials as a pastor; perhaps he has had his priorities out of sync all these years? Maybe he should have focused his efforts on building a good solid life for his wives and children rather than expending energy hating Fidel Castro.

Chapter 88
William Soler

On January 2, 1957 just a month after Castro and his men had returned from Mexico and two weeks before the first battle of the Revolution, tensions were running high in Santiago. Batista's police were looking for ways to intimidate people. Four young boys including William Soler were found dead in an empty building. They had been tortured and shot to death. William Soler had 1,000 thumb tacks pressed into his body. A Batista spy 'from the west' had accused them of being involved in revolutionary activities and the police were judge, jury, and executioner.

The identity of that spy from the west has never been known but a person of interest has arisen in the past two years among Cubans on the island – Rafael Bienvenido Cruz Diaz. If he was making US college plans in the fall of his senior year of high school (1956), he might have had to 'earn' the right to leave the country from the Batista regime. He did after all change his story from 'a friend of the family who was a lawyer bribed someone in the government to stamp my passport' to 'I convinced the Batista government to let me leave the country on a four year student visa.' My acquaintances in Cuba sketch this possible scenario involving Rafael Bienvenido Cruz Diaz.

Living in Matanzas, Rafael Bienvenido Cruz Diaz would have made a perfect undercover person to travel to Santiago and gather intelligence for Batista's police. Interior Minister Rafael Diaz Balart was known for using a network of young spies to try to keep tabs on the two large university student groups: AAA in Havana and FEU in Santiago.

On January 2, 1957 Rafael Bienvenido Cruz Diaz was on school Christmas Holiday and seven months from departing for the University of Texas. The Feast of Three Kings (important feast then in Cuba and now once again) was not until Sunday, January 6 so school would not have reopened until Monday, January7. Rafael Cruz could have easily traveled by train from Matanzas to Santiago, made false accusations against William Soler and the other boys and then returned home before school restarted.

This would have been an opportunity to earn 'cred' with the Batista government and 'convince them to let him leave the country on a four year student visa'. The Cuban national who developed this theory/scenario actually fought with Fidel Castro's rebels from the Sierra Maestra through 1959. The man is no slouch.

Though his health is now failing, he was sharp as a tack when we had the conversation regarding his theory about Rafael Bienvenido Cruz Diaz's possible involvement in William Soler's death.

Chapter 89

Frank Pais

Frank Pais was a young man who graduated from Oriente Teacher's College in Santiago de Cuba in July, 1953. When Fulgencio Batista executed his coup on March 10, 1952 Frank and other young people had gone to the Moncada Barracks to demand arms so that they could defend the democratic government of Carlos Prio Socarrás. They were turned away.

Shortly after Castro's attack on the Moncada barracks in Oriente Province in July 1953, Frank País began talking with students and young working people, men and women he knew personally, drawing them around him in an informal revolutionary group that became known as the Revolutionary National Action. País asked each person to organize a cell by preparing a list of their friends and close associates, people they could trust, to be members. These cells were composed of both students and workers from Santiago.

Cell members prepared carefully, finding, repairing, and hiding weapons, participating in mass demonstrations against the Batista government, raising

noney, and collecting medical supplies. They published a
ittle mimeographed bulletin which sold for ten cents,
eporting news and criticizing the government, countering
he censorship with which Batista periodically blanketed
he island.[148]

Pais' organization merged with the July 26
Movement (M-26-7) after Castro's release from jail. País
>ecame the leader of the new organization in Oriente
Province - FEU. Up to this moment neither the police in
Santiago nor the group members themselves knew the
extent of the organization País had so painstakingly built.

In early 1957, each cell was given the order to
paint the name of the movement along with anti-Batista
slogans on all the walls and buildings in their
neighborhood. The next morning the army, the police,
and the people of Santiago awoke to the magnitude of the
resistance. Every block in the city was covered with
writing splashed in paint; "Down with Batista! M-26-7!"
No one was arrested.

Pais would lead the four day uprising in Santiago
awaiting the arrival of Fidel Castro and his rebels from
Mexico aboard the yacht Granma. This is the event at

---

[148] Wikipedia Frank Pais

which Rafael Cruz falsely claimed to be leading a group of young fighters, being arrested and released when every other prisoner was being shot and killed.

Frank Pais escaped after the event and went into hiding. On June 30, 1957 Frank's younger brother, Josué Pais, was killed by the Santiago police in an attempt to flush Frank out for his funeral, but that strategy failed. He was however found by the Santiago police on July 30 hiding in a safe house. He was taken to a main thoroughfare in Santiago along with a companion and was tortured by police officers and then shot in the back of the head by Police Chief Jose Salas Canizares.

Many old time Cubans believe that if Frank Pais had lived he would probably have become the President of Cuba over Fidel Castro.

That Rafael Cruz would attempt to co-opt Frank Pais' heroics at Santiago de Cuba, and misrepresent the date of Pais' death is reprehensible. It is tantamount to the charlatans in the US who pretend they were in the military and claim to have been awarded medals.

Cuban Commentary: *This man is without a soul He is a priest; at what church, the church of the devil? -Yaneli, age 46 (Translated and edited for clarity)*

Chapter 90

Why Doesn't Rafael Cruz Hate the Rafael Diaz Balart Family – or Batista?

I've shown people in Cuba some of Rafael Cruz's videotaped speeches and some of Ted's speeches with translations. To a person they all trash the tall tales about he Revolution, torture, etc. Having seen a video of Ted elling the lies about his Aunt Sonia in a speech to the Cuban-American 'Mafia' in Miami[149], they raised a question – why would someone (the aunt) who had been tortured return to the scene of the crime?

In the video Ted Cruz praises both Lincoln Diaz Balart and his brother Mario Diaz Balart. They are sons of the late Rafael Diaz Balart who had been Batista's Interior Minister. If Rafael Cruz had truly been tortured, it would have been under the direction of Rafael Diaz Balart; how could Rafael Cruz allow his son Ted to associate with Diaz Balart's sons? Cubans claim that Rafael Diaz Balart ordered the execution of thousands of Batista opponents, and claim that he raped 74 school girls who'd been picked up by his goons to be turned over to US Mafia owned brothels.

---

[149] Lie # 51 and Lie # 52 videos

Having been told that Rafael Cruz often accompanies Ted Cruz on trips, the Cubans wondered if Rafael wasn't there in the audience glad handing with the sons of his alleged torture master.

The 'Miami Mafia' aka Center for a Free Cuba is comprised of all former Batistanis. They have been supporters of terrorists Orlando Bosch and Luis Posada Carilles, of terrorism, murder, arson, and other crimes. That Ted Cruz would go to Miami to address them and probably have his father in tow speaks volumes about the true relationship between the dregs of the Batista Dictatorship and Rafael and Ted Cruz. As president George W. Bush said in 2003, "If you give aid and comfort to a terrorist, you are a terrorist." By that measure, Ted Cruz is a terrorist.

And on another note, in all his speeches posted on You Tube, Rafael Cruz goes on and on about 'that bearded dictator I left behind', Fidel Castro. He only mentions Dictator Fulgencio Batista once: in Lie #15 when he talks about escaping to the mountains and the imaginary 'lady from the underground' tells him no. While he expresses deep hatred of Fidel Castro in every speech he comes off as deferential to Dictator Fulgencio Batista, the man whose thugs allegedly tortured him. That is truly puzzling. Would that be considered Stockholm Syndrome?

Chapter 91

Amorality in Cuban American Politicians & Why Cubans Fear Them

What is it about Batistani Cuban-American politicians that they must lie and deceive or act in immoral and criminal ways to get ahead? Senator Marco Rubio rose through the political ranks telling the story of how his parents escaped Castro's tyranny in 1959. When he was elected to the US Senate he was exposed as a liar by a reporter for the Washington Post. It was documented that his parents had in fact left Cuba in 1956 before the fighting began.

When Rubio was found to have charged personal expenses including auto repairs to a credit card issued to the Florida Republican Party for official party business, Marco Rubio's excuse was that he 'pulled the wrong credit card out of his wallet.' And this man wants to be elected President of the United States and be in control of the nuclear launch codes?

Robert Menendez the son of Cuban-American immigrants is under indictment for allegedly taking gifts and bribes from a doctor for whom Menendez did many political favors.

There are the principal remnants of the Batista Regime, the Diaz Balart Family. Their father, the late Rafael Diaz Balart was Batista's Interior Minister. He was over the military and police. Cubans despised him with such passion they wished he would have been returned to Cuba so they could have put him on trial for his alleged crimes. Mario Diaz Balart is a current member of the US Congress. His brother Lincoln (the smarter one according to Miami media) retired from Congress. After his father passed away Lincoln took his place as Cuban president-in-waiting in Havana North.

Then there is US Congresswoman Ileana Ros Lehtinen, the second most despised person in Cuba. Cubans claim that Ros Lehtinen's father Enrique was the 'bag man' for the Batista Dictatorship – he went around collecting kickbacks and protection money from the American owners of casinos and brothels.

In first place as most despised person in Cuba is the murderous terrorist who Congresswoman Ros Lehtinen has protected from prosecution for 25 years, Luis Posada Carilles. He was one of two masterminds who blew Cubana Airlines Flt 455 out of the sky on

October 6, 1976 killing 78, including the young members of the Cuban National Fencing Team.

Congresswoman Ros Lehtinen also protected his co-terrorist who has since passed away, terrorist Orlando Bosch. She also protected Posada from being extradited for the Havana Tourist bombings in 1997, and then again in 2005.

Cuban-American terrorism is still alive and well in South Florida. In March 2012 a group of 305 Miami-area pilgrims traveled to Cuba for the Masses celebrated by Pope Benedict XVI. One month after they returned the travel agency that booked the group was firebombed in the middle of the night. It was in close proximity to Congresswoman Ros Lehtinen's office in Coral Gables.

This act of terrorism took place on the one year anniversary of the death of the godfather of Cuban-American terrorism, Orland Bosch. The FBI and ATF arrived and took samples but never returned with any results. Readers can draw their own conclusions as to why they were called off the case. The local Fire Marshal ruled it arson.

These thugs and their lies are reinforced by Cuban-American members of the media. The Diaz Balart clan has their brother Jose who is an anchor for

Telemundo and MSNBC. His slant on all news Cuban is apparent. Then there is Mario Loyola, the sycophant who filed the story with *National Review Online* enabling the lying by Rafael Cruz and trashing the *Dallas Morning News* for questioning Cruz's credibility. The Miami (Havana North) Herald is a mouthpiece for the Batistanis.

Cubans are well aware of Congresswoman Ros Lehtinen's role as a supporter of terrorism. They believe that she orchestrated Luis Posada's trip to Cuba in 1997 to bomb tourist destinations, and they also believe she is the mastermind behind the Coral Gables 2012 bombing which was widely reported in Cuba. They accuse her of being the ringleader of the group that tried to kidnap Elian Gonzales in 1999.

The average man in Cuba despises US Congresswoman Ileana Ros Lehtinen. He will tell you if she ever stepped off a plane in Havana he would go at her with a machete. He would also tell you that he fears her. He is willing to speak and share thoughts and insights but he insists on remaining anonymous for fear of Congresswoman Ileana Ros Lehtinen dispatching another one of her terrorist allies to Cuba to do him harm.

Even the housewives who agreed to be photographed for inclusion in this book and the parents of 'oung girls who agreed to have their daughters photos ncluded all insisted on their faces being hidden because hey fear being targeted for assassination by Congresswoman Ileana Ros Lehtinen, her protégé Senator Marco Rubio, or by the two sons of the brutal Batista Interior Minister, Rafael Diaz Balart.

Cuban Commentary: *"Ileana Ros sent Posada Carilles here to bomb the hotels and tourist centers to kill people in 1997. She could easily send someone here to kill me. Please do not use my real name in your book Please cover my wife's face in her picture. God Bless you Paulo."* - *Raul, age 43 (Translated and edited for clarity)*

Chapter 92

So proud to be an American

48 years late, with a long term gig as a proud Canadian – which got him in on that government's Socialized Medicine

At some point in every speech when he's talking about his 'escape' from Cuba in 1957 or about the return from his imaginary trip in 1959, Rafael Cruz goes all fife and drum and proclaims, "I was so lucky to be able to come to the land of the free and the home of the brave. I am so proud to be an American."[150] (With a heavy Spanish accent; Press '1' to hear that statement spoken clearly by his son Ted)

He arrived in Texas in August, 1957. He did not become a US citizen until 2005. Why the 48 year wait? Could it be that he was part of the Miami Cartel headed by Jorge Mas Canosa and then Rafael Diaz Balart, the two fantasy Cuban presidents-in-waiting who have since gone to their final reward?

When Diaz Balart the former Batista Interior Minister passed away in 2005, the title of fantasy Cuban president-in-waiting passed to his son Lincoln Diaz

---

[150] https://www.youtube.com/watch?v=W0HTEUyVWK4

Balart. Perhaps Rafael Cruz figured his time had passed with that fantasy so he decided to become a US citizen at age 66 to get on the US government's gravy train for senior citizens.

The strange wrinkle is the fact that he became a Canadian citizen before becoming an American. This occurred during the handful of years that he lived in Canada where he fled with his second wife after abandoning his first wife and two daughters. This was also where he became a fast living alcoholic according to his son Ted Cruz and where he would eventually abandon his second wife and his little son Raffy.

Canada is where little Raffy Cruz was born. Of course when Raffy was born in 1970, Canada's Socialized medicine was for Canadian citizens only. Foreigners had to pay cash for medical treatments. I learned that first hand when I broke my ankle in Niagara Falls in 1975.

Although he claims to have become a self-made millionaire Rafael Cruz did not want to have to pay out of pocket for little Raffy's birth and any aftercare for him or the Baby Mama. So the quick thinking Rafael Cruz who dreamt up the idea of attending school in the US while still freshly tortured in 1957 put his thinking cap on and thought, "I know, I'll become a Canadian citizen before we have our baby and then these suckers – the Canadian taxpayers – can foot the bill. I deserve a handout; after all I was tortured and beaten half to death and then fled oppression. I'm going to take advantage of Trudeaucare."

How ironic. I am not going to post clips because readers are tired of listening to this old man's lies but in speech after speech he trashes 'Socialized medicine' in Cuba, Canada, Great Britain, and anywhere else that the government helps tend to the well-being of its citizens. He spits nails when he trashes Obamacare and the Black president behind it.

Yet Rafael Cruz went to the trouble (not much trouble actually, less cumbersome process than the US) to become a Canadian citizen so that he could be a parasite and bleed free healthcare. Isn't that a bite in the butt as my father used to say?

It begs the question: was there something preventing Rafael Cruz and his second wife from returning to the United States to have their son born on US soil? Could Rafael Cruz have been ducking his first wife and two daughters? Custody issues; perhaps unpaid child support? He and Raffy's Baby Mama would have only had to come back for a short period of time. Rafael

Cruz was a multi-millionaire; it would not have been cost prohibitive to travel back to the US. Perhaps there would have been concern about a pregnant woman flying on an airplane. That's why God gave us automobiles. It was only a 3 hour drive from Calgary to the US border in Montana, and another two hours to Great Falls.

There is also the possibility that Rafael Cruz may have been 'hiding out' in Canada, especially given his dark character and lack of truthfulness. Most felony crimes in Texas have a statute of limitations of five to seven years.[151] Rafael Cruz has never stated exactly how long he was in Canada but it was from approximately 1967 to 1974, a period of seven years. The Texas criminal code contains the types of crimes that would have a seven year statute of limitations most of which involve financial fraud and tax crimes. These are certainly crimes that in my opinion a dishonest individual like Rafael Cruz would be capable of committing.

On Monday, June 29 Ted Cruz was on the Today Show whining about the 'unelected justices on the US Supreme Court who cannot be recalled'. He was arguing that they should be elected and subject to recall. That is what Texas has with its state supreme court and it is

---

[151] Texas Criminal Code – Limitations, Felonies (Sec 12.01)

arguably the most corrupt in the US, for sale to the highest bidder.

Cruz was lamenting the decision legalizing same sex marriage, calling it 'some of the darkest 24 hours in US history'. When Savannah Guthrie asked him if his position didn't amount to discrimination he replied, "I'm the son of a Cuban immigrant who fled oppression. I know about discrimination." What? Cubans have an express lane to green cards and citizenship on their arrival, provided they pledge their loyalty to the three Cuban American terrorists in Congress, Ileana Ros Lehtinen, Mario Diaz Balart, and Marco Rubio.[152]

On Tuesday, June 30 he stated on the Hugh Hewitt radio show, "I am the son of a Cuban immigrant who had been imprisoned and tortured and fled oppression to come to this country." It is a safe bet that will be his recurring theme of his presidential campaign as it was his US Senate campaign in 2012.

But as usual, Ted Cruz's lips were moving so he was lying in both instances. He is not the son of a Cuban immigrant. He is the son of a Canadian immigrant.

---

[152] In 2003 President George W. Bush said, "If you give aid and comfort to a terrorist you are a terrorist," These three have done that going back to 1990, protecting men who were labeled by the FBI the most dangerous terrorists in the Western Hemisphere

Chapter 93

Was Ted Cruz an illegitimate child?

There are so many convoluted lies in the narratives told by Rafael Cruz and Ted Cruz. All are designed to make the two look like honorable men of God, men who have always walked the straight and narrow in fear of God. But when you peel back the layers of the onion, strange facts raise troubling questions.

It's known that in his senior year of studies at the University of Texas Rafael Cruz got a young lady pregnant and they had a daughter in November, 1961. It is also a fact that just shy of one year later they had a second daughter in November, 1962. There is no record in Texas in Travis, Dallas, or Harris counties of Rafael Bienvenido Crus Diaz being divorced.

There are various tales of how or when Rafael Cruz came to live in Calgary. He was obviously there on December 22, 1970 when his son Rafael Edward Cruz was born. He was living there with the former Eleanor Darragh. Rafael Edward Cruz's birth certificate issued by the Department of Health, Division of Vital Statistics in

Edmonton, Alberta No. 70-08-032264 lists Rafael
Edward Cruz's mother as Eleanor Elizabeth Wilson.[153]

That was Ted Cruz's mother's name with her first
husband who she had apparently left before taking up
with Rafael Cruz. If she put her married name on Ted's
birth certificate, was she not married to Rafael
Bienvenido Cruz, the person listed as the father?

Was Ted Cruz born out of wedlock to the man
who degrades single young mothers? Rafael Cruz falsely
claimed that taking Bible reading and prayer out of
schools in 1963 caused teen pregnancy to skyrocket. We
know that the truth is just the opposite. But could the
removal of prayer and Bible study have led to an increase
in adultery and fornication out of wedlock?

.

---

[153] Rafael Edward Cruz birth certificate - Appendix

Epilogue

Watching and listening to Rafael Cruz is both sickening and frightening. He is a very dark man. He never smiles, not even when he makes an attempt at a joke. My mother used to say about a person who does not smile: 'the devil lives in him.' One might feel the need to take a shower after watching his videos. I call them political pornography: deviant, warped, and twisted.

Rafael Cruz certainly gets angry; he's the old man screaming from his porch only he is at a podium with an audience full of gullible people hanging on the pastor's every word.

When Rafael Cruz mentions President Obama the veins bulge in his neck. I suspect Rafael Cruz still resents Fidel Castro for opening up education and job opportunities for Blacks and women.

Ironically, for a self-proclaimed Constitutional Conservative he never criticizes Harry Reid, Nancy Pelosi, Ruth Bader Ginsburg, Stephen Breyer, Elena Kagan, or Sonia Sotomayor. The biggest difference between these individuals and President Obama is their skin color; perhaps that's why they escape his wrath.

There are dozens and dozens of videos on You Tube of Rafael Cruz giving speeches. With some variation, they are usually all the same – and they are all full of lies and full of hate – mostly for President Obama. Watching them becomes disgusting, like watching old KKK rallies.

What is especially peculiar is that for a man with a massive ego Rafael Cruz is a stealth character. He has neither website nor publicist, but does have a Facebook page where people praise him and label him 'First Papa 2017'. His FB page lists no appearances before the fact. Rafael Cruz seems to want to avoid any media presence at his appearances, lest he be questioned and challenged as to the veracity of his stories.

Rafael Cruz is a one man jihad. He wants to turn the United States into a theocracy, with his own version of Sharia Law and he has declared war on Socialist/Marxist/Communist/Comrade Barak Obama. Sharia comes from the Quran; Rafael Cruz wants all US laws to come from the Old Testament. (We can take care of homosexual marriage; stone the homosexuals)

Rafael Cruz demands that there be a voter registration table in every church in America. A frequent quote from Rafael Cruz: "It's time that this country stops

•eing politically correct and starts being Biblically
:orrect."

Rafael Cruz mentions Karl Marx more than he
mentions his alleged torturer Batista. He claims that
Marxists say whatever they have to in order to advance
heir cause. He should look inward and reflect on that
statement.

Rafael Cruz probably resents Jimmy Carter
because Carter allowed the Mariel Boatlift to take place.
This brought many Afro-Cubans to Miami but over the
past 30 years the Cuban-American diaspora in Miami
have cleansed the community of dark-skinned people.
Rare is it to see an Afro-Cuban in South Florida; they
have moved on elsewhere.

Rafael Cruz rails about 'hyphenated Americans
like African-Americans' yet he and his son are all so cozy
with the hyphenated population of Cuban-Americans in
South Florida.

The Cruz men are in my opinion political
predators. How do predators lure their victims? They
flatter and charm them ('I am so proud to be with such a
group of patriots'), they tell stories that cause people to
empathize with them (arrest and torture/Dad walked out
on Mom and me until he was saved), and once they earn

the victim's trust they abuse them. Rafael Cruz primarily and Ted Cruz to a lesser extent have abused their audiences psychologically with horrific lies. View the plethora of Rafael Cruz You Tube Videos, listen to the people fawning over Rafael Cruz, buying his lies, and then standing and pledging Rafael Cruz' oath.

Rafael Cruz did not grow up and take responsibility for his life until 1979 when he was 40 years old, supposedly becoming a Texas board member of the Religious Roundtable and becoming a player in Ronald Reagan's 1980 Campaign. Living the American Dream? It was more like Rafael Cruz driving the American Nightmare.

Rafael Cruz's favorite catch line in his speeches is 'as a matter of fact'. How ironic since most of his facts are self-manufactured.

In April 2015 Rafael Cruz added the following line to his script: "My son Ted Cruz for President. He will tell the truth." Has Ted Cruz ditched Rafael Cruz and found a new mentor, one with integrity and a moral compass who will guide him to tell the truth, unlike his fraud father?

How can Rafael Cruz's audiences be so gullible? Cram 24 hours of food into yourself in eight hours? Learn o master the English language by sitting in a theater watching movies for a month? How can anyone buy such idiculous gibberish? What does that say about the intellectual capacity of Tea Party members, or their desperation for someone to look up to?

Finally, Rafael Cruz is always introduced as pastor or reverend, and as a professor of the Bible and theology. Oddly though Rafael Cruz himself never mentions any of these titles; he only refers to himself as a scientist when trashing the theory of Evolution. A Google search of Rafael Cruz, Rafael Bienvenido Cruz, or Rafael B. Cruz only brings up article and You Tube videos which are all politically oriented. Nothing comes up about any religious affiliations or activities by this so-called man of God. To say that this man is the biggest con artist in US political history is an understatement.

The Torch is Passed

I can honestly say I have never encountered anyone in my life that lies like Rafael Bienvenido Cruz Oh sure I've met liars in bars, on airplanes, at business events who whipped up a tale of two. As a professional sales trainer I myself have spun some tales, but in the role of fabulist so that I could drive home a point in a sales class.

At age 76 there is no knowing how long the Energizer Bunny of lies will continue to move his lips. However his legacy is entrenched through his progeny, Rafael Edward Cruz. His lips have been moving quite aggressively in the United States Senate and they no doubt will ramp up in his campaign for the GOP nomination for president.

But Rafael Edward Cruz has already set a high bar of dishonesty and deception in his commenting to an audience about a bill introduced by Senators Chuck Schumer and Tom Udall. The bill proposes a Constitutional Amendment to override the Supreme Court ruling in Citizens United which said that corporations are people and people can spend as much as they want on a political campaign for a candidate of their

reference.[154] Rafael II tells the crowd that the bill is for

n amendment to repeal the First Amendment to the US

Constitution. He even throws in the liar's disclaimer –

folks I'm not making this up' though he is.

The bill does not seek to repeal the First

Amendment – it only seeks to limit the amount of money

hat corporations and billionaires can spend to buy the

mouths of political prostitutes.

---

[154] https://www.youtube.com/watch?v=fBn07MYfN30

This Is Such a Crock of . . . ![155]
Excerpts from

A Time for Truth
Ted Cruz
Released June 30, 2015

When I heard that Ted Cruz was releasing a book in late June comically titled *A Time for Truth* I just knew it would contain more Ted Cruz lies. Ted did not disappoint; Ted Cruz and Rafael Cruz are like crack cocaine addicts when it comes to fabricating lies – try as they might the egotistical high they get from lying is just too powerful for the Cruz men to seek a twelve step program for their addictions.

"My name is Ted, and I am a pathological liar." Group responds: "Hello Ted!" "My nem ees Rafael, and I too am a pasholoyical lieyar." Group responds: "Bienvenido Rafael." Look of shock: "How eet ess you know my miyyle name? " There are two women in the Cruz world who might be able to facilitate an intervention for these two pathological liars:. Ted's mother and Rafael's second ex-wife Eleanor Darragh and Ted's wife Heidi Nelson Cruz.

---

[155] Colonel Frank Slade, played by Al Pacino, Scent of a Woman, 193

Though it's extremely odd that the only publicly
identified photos of Eleanor Darragh are the ones in A
Time for Truth all from before 1975. Is Ted embarrassed
to have his photo taken with his Mom other than one at 4
years old? Lord knows the web is full of photos of him
and his lying coach Rafael. No doubt Eleanor has little
use for Rafael Cruz; when she divorced her first husband
she kept his last name 'Wilson', even listing it as her last
name on Ted's Calgary birth certificate when she was
supposedly married to Rafael. But she left the Cruz name
at the courthouse door in Harris County, Texas in 1997
when Pastor Rafael Cruz was granted his divorce from
her.

Another interesting photograph (on the web) is
from election night 2012 when Ted Cruz won the US
Senate Race. Victorious candidates (even losers) always
stand hip to hip with their spouse. But a photo of the
celebration shows Ted Cruz holding one of his daughters,
and a woman to his right holding the other daughter (his
mother perhaps?), Rafael Cruz attached to Ted at the hip,
and Ted's wife Heidi standing away from her husband
with Rafael Cruz wedged between them and Heidi with
her head bowed. For God's chosen 'first family' this
certainly is an odd group.

But the point of this chapter is Ted Cruz's whopping crock of warm, steamy sh** in *A Time for Truth*. Honestly I am tired of reviewing video and written lies by these two con men and were I to cover every lie in Ted Cruz's book I would double my page count.

There are however two lies that I want to cover; one that is proof positive of what amoral liars the Cruz men are and how they don't care whose valor they steal to improve their images. A second lie which illustrates how Ted Cruz is so desperate to build up his and his father's egos that he will steal the story line from a Hollywood movie channeling an Academy Award winning performance to his father and co-opting for himself the role of one of the 1990's brightest young male stars.

`Let's begin with Ted Cruz's first disgusting lie. In Chapters 37 and 90 we discussed at length Frank Pais, a young leader of the university student movement who organized university students in Oriente Province and who let the 300 students to Santiago to support Fidel Castro's arrival from Mexico with his rebels. On Page 12 of his book,

Ted Cruz claims his father left his revolutionary cell in Matanzas in September 1956, traveled 830

;ilometers and enrolled at the University of Santiago in
September, 1956. This was fortuitous because at that
point Castro hadn't yet decided in which coastal location
he was going to land: Pinar del Rio, Playa Giron (Bay of
Pigs), or Santiago. Ted Cruz further states that his father
reported to Frank Pais and then was part of the support
team for Castro when he arrived from Mexico on
December 2. Cuban American writer Mario Loyola wrote
of his interview with Rafael in National Review Online
that 'Rafael had risen to a position of leadership by this
time.'[156]

My contacts in Cuba including an octogenarian
who fought with Castro and his rebels told me this week
this scenario is highly unlikely. "Why would he have
enrolled at University of Santiago? If the story were
accurate it would have made more sense to enroll at the
University of Oriente which was Pais' school and base of
operations." My Cuban friend says it is highly unlikely
that Pais and his team would have taken in a boy who just
arrived from 830 kilometers away. He could have been a
spy sent by Interior Minister Rafael Diaz Balart and his
favorite assassins the Masferrer Brothers.

---

[156] Exile and the Revolution, 11-4-11 Mario Loyola

But Ted Cruz goes over the top when he claims that all of the student members of 26th of July Movement who were there to support Castro's return in Frank Pais' group were killed, *including their leader Frank Pais.*[157]

Fank Pais did not die in battle on December 2, 1956. This is a lie told to me on video by Rafael Cruz back in June, 2013 in Weatherford, Texas and written by Ted Cruz into his sarcastically titled book *A Time for Truth* (Cruz Truth?) Frank Pais escaped on December 2 and was eventually arrested and tried for the Santiago incident; he was acquitted and released. He went into hiding but he was the target of Interior Minister Rafael Diaz Balart. Diaz Balart's police searched high and low but could not locate him.

On June 30, 1957 Frank's younger brother Josue Pais was murdered by the Santiago police. They had hoped to flush Frank out of hiding to attend his brother's funeral but Frank did not bite. A systematic search of the city was implemented and on July 30 the police found Frank hiding out with a friend. They were dragged into the street, tortured by police officers, and then the chief of police shot him in the head and killed him. The next day 60,000 people attended his funeral, forcing the city to be shut down. This was eight months after Ted Cruz claims in his book *A Time for Truth* that Frank Pais was killed..

---

[157] A Time for Truth, Ted Cruz, page 13

Today Frank Pais is a hero in Cuba. Many schools nd public facilities and hospitals bear his name. The nternational airport in Holguin, Cuba is named after him. School children learn of his heroics. And what happened o the cowardly pathological liar Rafael Cruz during the ncident in Santiago? Was Rafael Cruz one of the many ourageous students and young revolutionaries who were illed? No; it's probably likely he was home with his amily in Matanzas with visions of sugar plums and ventually of American rubias (blonde girls) on the UT campus dancing in his head.

Santiago was in turmoil. The military were hunting Castro and his surviving rebels. The police were hunting surviving members of Frank Pais Group M26-7 with their distinctive olive green uniforms with red and black armbands. (Which Rafael Cruz claims in Chapter 38 never existed)

Ted Cruz claims that Rafael and his friends were leaving the city by car (teenagers with a car; affluent families for sure - no doubt chilling to the sounds of Tito Puente or Desi Arnaz) and were stopped and taken prisoner by the military. They were being driven by the soldiers to the Moncada Barracks, the soldiers shouting 'firing squad, firing squad.' But miraculously, God had other plans for Rafael Cruz, eventually fathering 'the chosen one' after abandoning a wife and two daughters.

As for Rafael and his posse cruising out of the
city and then being taken to the firing squads, my friend
in Cuba for the first time asked me to reiterate
information that I had sent because it seemed to be an
incredible example of incredible facts. He tells me that
was not the case. Diaz Balart's personal assassins the
Masferrer Brothers, the police, and soldiers simply lined
captives up and walked down the line shooting them in
the head. They enjoyed the thrill of brain matter and
blood splattering in front of a point blank shot. (Similar to
the current ISIS beheading method) This was efficient;
firing squads took too long.

For the second outrageous lie I wish to address,
well as Pastor Rafael Cruz would say, "God has our lives
ordered." I consider myself to be a Guy's Guy; and what
is a favorite past time of guy's guys? Quoting movies
lines; often times from silly sophomoric movies *(Caddy
Shack, Austin Powers, Ted 2)* but sometimes serious
movies with major life lessons such as *Shawshank
Redemption* and *Scent of a Woman.*

Scent of a Woman (1993) is my favorite all time
movie because it is a great life lesson for young men and
it earned an Academy Award for my favorite actor Al
Pacino. I had my two sons watch it with their friends as
they matured through high school. As for Al Pacino, not
only is he incredibly talented but he is entwined in the

ustory of my hometown of Woonsocket, Rhode Island.
n 1961 as a budding young actor he and friends were
topped by the local police for suspicious driving wearing
nasks and gloves. A .38 was found in the vehicle trunk
and the men could not post bond so they spent three
ughts in jail. [158]

So Imagine my surprise in perusing *A Time for
Truth* when I got to page 46 and began to read a story that
- to paraphrase Law and Order: SVU – was ripped from a
movie storyline. In Scent of a Woman there are parallel
story lines: Colonel Frank Slade (Al Pacino)
contemplating the ending of his life, and Charlie Simms
(Chris O'Donnell) a scholarship student from Oregon
coming of age at an exclusive WASP prep school in New
England.

Charlie faces a huge dilemma. He witnessed three
fellow students commit a criminal act of vandalism
directed at the school headmaster which humiliated the
headmaster before the entire student body. The
headmaster tries to force Charlie to rat out on his school
mates (crass rich kids, not friends). Mr. Trask even tries
to bribe Charlie with a guaranteed admission to Harvard.
Charlie holds firm and in a student body assembly he is
dressed down by Trask who threatens expulsion, calling
Simms a 'cover-up artist and a liar.'

---

[158] http://www.famouslyarrested.com/actors/al-pacino.html

At that point, Colonel Slade who had gone to the Baird School to support Charlie *in loco parentis* (in place of the parents) finally chimes in. "But not a snitch! This is such a crock of shit!" Pacino then goes on to support Charlie in one of the most amazing monologues from a movie ever.

'*Rafael and Ted's Excellent Adventure*' at Second Baptist School, a school for rich kids[159] in Houston, Texas involved one of the oldest school pranks in the book, and one that was perpetrated against my family several times because I had two sons in sports. 'T-P-ing' a house, or trees - decorating someone's property with toilet paper.

In conjunction with Second Baptist's Homecoming, a rival school had stolen the school flag from the campus. So channeling his Cuban revolutionary father Rafael Commander Cruz put together a plan of retaliation. Here is what he writes on page 46: "Outraged, I assembled a group of three other students to avenge this wrong. We drove to Northwest Academy in my car, a 1978 green Ford Fairmont given to me by my grandfather. We called it the Green Bomb. And it was a wonderful car to give to a teenage boy because it was

---

[159] '15 – '16 cost $18,780 tuition + purchase of books and supplies http://www.secondbaptistschool.org/Page/ADMISSIONS/Affording-SBS

basically a tank a very large hunk of metal that got about ten miles to the gallon."

At this point I must digress because we're not talking about a garden variety liar here; we are talking about pathological incessant liar Ted Cruz. Here is what Ford Motor Company said about their 1978 Ford Fairmont:

The Ford Fairmont is a mid-size car produced for the North American market that was sold from the 1978 to the 1983 model years. Introduced as the successor to the Maverick, the Fairmont was sold by Lincoln-Mercury dealers as the Mercury Zephyr. The Fairmont and Zephyr were sold as two-door notchback sedans, two-door coupes, and four-door sedan.

The Fairmont and Zephyr marked the introduction of the long-running Ford Fox platform, used for a wide variety of later models. The hallmark of this platform in the post Oil Embargo of the mid-1970's was its smaller design and use of lightweight components to increase fuel efficiency to over 25 miles per gallon.

While retaining a conventional rear-wheel drive platform, the Fairmont was efficiently packaged and offered excellent passenger and cargo room for its size. Contemporary reviews uniformly praised the Rack-and-pinion steering gave the Fairmont much better handling and roadability than its Maverick predecessor and despite its roomier interior, lightweight components were used which gave the Fairmont better fuel economy than the Maverick.

As Ford switched to lighter, more aerodynamic cars with front-wheel drive in the 1980s, the Fairmont was replaced by the all-new Tempo for 1984

Pardon me for making that automotive detour, (pun intended) but it is important to illustrate Ted Cruz's capacity for lying. (Perhaps he is trying to paint a picture of he and his three amigos barreling along in a big old tank, just like Rafael and his Compadres who were fleeing Santiago) How can you tell when Ted Cruz is lying – his court stenographer has blisters on her fingers.

Back to our movie knock-off. Ted claims he and and his posse ran to the grocery store and buy thirty-six rolls of toilet paper, shaving cream, toothpaste, and baby shampoo. They then headed to their rival school and T-P-ed a building! Oh the Humanity! They brought toilet paper that would dissipate in any rainstorm. They brought shaving cream which they used to 'paint' funny faces on the school bus windows. They brought toothpaste and baby shampoo for unexplained reasons.

We are not talking about trashing the headmaster's new Jaguar (*Scent of a Woman*). This event might have been considered an act of benevolence to get the student body energized. Now we have a slight difference here: Charlie Simms observed the act of vandalism; Ted Cruz was the ringleader. Well of course.

Do you think that Ted Cruz, who I believe suffers from Narcissistic Personality Disorder would settle for the role of voyeur? Hell no! 'Rafelito' or 'Felito'[160] as he was known to his family had to be leader of the gang!

He was after all the progeny of a hero of the Cuban Revolution who was arrested, almost killed twice, tortured, beaten half to death, daringly outfoxed Batista's goons and sailed to America with $100 hidden in his sweaty underwear. He had to 'lay a foundation' in lawyer-speak to be able to weave a web of lies so he could come off as a pseudo hero, conning the suckers who P.T. Barnum says are born every minute.

The janitors at Northwest chased the Green Bomb and wrote down the license plate and complained to the Second Baptist principal Mr. Doss.[161] Mr. Doss called Ted in and being a stand-up guy, Ted admitted his role in the non-dastardly act. And like Mr. Trask at the Baird School, Mr. Doss wanted what is known in horseracing as a Superfecta – The *Four Horsemen of the Apocalypse* in a line one behind the other crossing his finish line.

---

[160] A Time for Truth, Page 34
[161] Ibid, Page 45

"Well then, tell me who was with you," Mr. Doss demanded of our hero, who replied: "Sir I already told you, I think it would be in poor character and contrary to my integrity to give you those names, and I'm not going to do so."

Ted wasn't about to break. Mr. Doss hadn't even kicked his teeth out, this after all wasn't Cuba. But he could have tried a beating with a pillow case filled with oranges. Rafael II was gonna show Mr. Doss and especially Rafael I what a tough guy he was. After all, the plantain doesn't fall far from the tree. Rafael I might even have been planning to have Mama sew money into Ted's underwear when he went off to college.

Like Mr. Trask at Baird, Mr. Doss played the Ivy League card. Ted had been accepted at Princeton. He slowly opened his desk drawer (cue dramatic music) pulled out a letter and handed it to Ted to read. It was to the president of Princeton asking that Ted's acceptance be rescinded! Knock a kid with arguably a promising future out of Princeton over toilet paper and toothpaste? This wasn't Baird which has educated ambassadors, Cabinet members, foreign prime ministers, among many luminaries. Second Baptist's most notable alumnus was

Nathan Morris, R & B Singer in Boys II Men[162]. Ted
Cruz was the first Ivy League acceptance in school
history.

Mr. Doss then said, "We're going to call your
father." Helpful lad, Ted wrote down his father's number.
Mr. Doss called and spoke with Rafael. We don't know if
Rafael channeled Al Pacino and stated, "But he's not a
snitch! This is such a crock of shit! Where's the booze?
It's flowing like mud around here."

Mr. Doss handed the phone to Ted. He claims that
Rafael told his son, "you only have a few months to
graduate, stick to your guns. I'm proud of you."

Ted stuck to his guns. The principal then
brought in Ted's three amigos. The principal knew all
along who they were. Ted claimed it was all a test to
make him buckle to teach him a lesson but it failed.
Perhaps there is something to be said for 7 x 7 foot cells,
1000 watt bulbs, beatings, and kicking someone's teeth
out.

There were only two witnesses to this alleged
conversation, Rafael Edward 'Felito' Cruz and Principal
Doss. God's light shines on Ted Cruz; lucky for him Mr.
Doss is deceased; so unless he maintained a Nixon-like

---

[162] www.secondbaptistschool.org

recording system in his office there is no one to validate or refute the story, except for common sense. Of course since this event occurred in 1988 and Scent of a Woman did not come out until 1993 I could see sycophants like Mario Loyola and Bob Weir claiming that screenwriter Bo Goldman overheard Ted boasting about the event in a bar near Princeton or Harvard and stole the story from Ted Cruz.

Ted Cruz: Loving Parent or Narcissist?

When Cruz talks of his daughter Caroline's birth ne manages to hammer out 42 words. He doesn't discuss Catherine's birth but he does give her 44 words talking about her encounter with Joe Biden at Ted's US Senate swearing in ceremony, an incident that made it into *Time Magazine's Notable Quotes.*

Ever the NRA mouthpiece he mentions both girls and his wife in a 25 word sentence about how if anyone ever entered his home trying to injure them, 'they would encounter a very direct exercise of his Second Amendment rights.' Slim chance – the family lives in a luxury high-rise penthouse in Houston.

And finally we all remember his non-filibuster filibuster on the Senate floor that ran October 24 -25 2013 and lasted 21 hours and 19 minutes. This was where he used his daughters as props by reading a Bible story (would you expect anything less from a faux Evangelical) and Dr. Seuss' *Green Eggs and Ham* to Caroline and Catherine via C-SPAN.

He devoted a whopping 18 words to recounting the event. He was more generous in recounting Caroline's eventual feedback – 51 words. If you weren't keeping track I was: The Senator and Presidential Candidate's two cherubic daughters generated 180 words in the entire book.

In describing how nervous he was about possibly being deselected from Princeton, Ted went on and on about what attending the Ivy League institution would mean to him, giving a litany of alumni and their various works that he admired. He devoted 186 words describing what Princeton meant to him, but only 180 words to his daughters.

Look up narcissist in the dictionary and guess whose mug will be looking out at you? But in defense of Ted Cruz, how much can you lie about two sweet little girls? I mean beyond when you say 'they got right up to the television and giggled with glee' you state emphatically that they were 'in their pink PJs' when the photo in the center of Ted's book clearly shows them wearing lime green PJs.

Perhaps the PJs were similar to 'The Dress' that went viral on the internet this year, the one that looked different colors to different people.

Does this seem petty, criticizing Ted Cruz for a minor mistruth about the color of pajamas when you compare it to the volume of major lies he has fabricated?

Perhaps but I use it to illustrate a point. Shouldn't someone who argues before the Supreme Court of the United States be a stickler for details? How about someone who wants to be president of the United States? Details count, and while we are at it, honesty does as well.

It calls to mind another Cuban-American Senator, Marco Rubio of Florida who is loyal to mass murderers and terrorists who he helps protect from prosecution. When he was Speaker of the Florida House he was given an Amex card by the state GOP for official business.[163] He used it to pay all kinds of personal expenses including a $120 haircut (manscaping for the little man maybe?) auto rental, a family vacation to Disney World, and car repairs. When he was caught and asked to explain, he said he 'picked up the wrong credit card to pay.' What? Details, details, details, Marco; can't you put your little fingers on the right piece of plastic?

His Amex records also showed he paid travel for 10 trips for a young Florida healthcare lobbyist named Amber Stoner to travel with him.[164] What's his excuse

---

[163] http://www.tampabay.com/news/politics/legislature/records-show-marco-rubio-spent-thousands-with-gop-credit-card/1075692
[164] http://www.motherjones.com/politics/2012/04/ten-things-you-need-know-about-marco-rubio

there? Picked up the right credit card but went off with the wrong woman; went off with Amber Stoner instead of his wife, former Miami Dolphins Cheerleader Jeanette Dousdebe?[165]

I cannot tell a lie – there was a time in my life I would have loved to travel ten times to resort hotels with a woman named *Stoner* especially with Florida Republicans footing the bill! So I might have a little Marco envy. But it is obvious that neither he nor Ted Cruz possesses the honesty, integrity, or attention to detail to be president of the United States.

I know two Cuban-Americans of impeccable character who would make fine future presidents. Jhon Cores currently a 24 year old teaching assistant at North Carolina State University, and six year old Julian Willis son of a wonderful set of parents Isabel Alfonso and Ben Willis who makes his home in New York.

I was also struck by a symbol of narcissism on the cover *of A Time for Truth (this is after all, Ted Cruz)* that is worth noting. Most books that line the shelves of bookstores have a prominent title with the author's name less prominent. (Go ahead look at this book's cover)

---

[165] http://www.ibtimes.com/who-marco-rubios-wife-jeanette-desdoubes-former-miami-dolphins-cheerleader-shies-away-1877823

The most prominent type on the cover of the book by TED CRUZ is his name. The title is in smaller font. The only thing that overshadows the narcissist's name on the cover is the narcissist's picture. I wonder how many autographed copies he has given *himself?*

In the 1980's a lady friend who worked for a Boston bank asked me to accompany her to a cocktail party on the yacht Trump Princess moored at Boston's Commonwealth Pier. The Donald arrived by helicopter and we all went aboard to enjoy cocktails and hors d'oeuvres. Every magazine cover he had ever been on adorned the walls, blown up in size. No Ivana, no children, just The Donald in every state room and public area.

At the time of this writing Ted Cruz had come out in defense of Trump calling Mexican immigrants criminals, drug dealers, and rapists.[166] This shows that there is honor among thieves, honor among liars, and honor among narcissists.

And because Ted Cruz is the gift that keeps on giving I will cite one other matter that I caught on television on Sunday July 5, 2015. I happened to pass by

---

[166] http://www.theguardian.com/us-news/2015/jul/02/donald-trump-racist-claims-mexico-rapes

the Spanish language cable network Univision. Ted Cruz was being interviewed by host Jorge Ramos. There was something about Ted Cruz that appeared different, but just what was it? Wait a minute, I see what it is. In all other videos, whether they are from You Tube, media outlets or the Cruz campaign, Ted Cruz always has a pasty white face.

Here on Univision, Ted Cruz is brown! Wow! I knew in the old days they had what was known as 'blackface' make-up; but brownface? Is that a way to woo the Hispanic vote? A better way might be to speak Spanish, especially if he wants to claim the mantle of Hispanic candidate on Spanish language cable network.

Judge for yourself readers; view the video showing the many faces of Ted Cruz. [167]

Ted Cruz is the gift that keeps on giving. Watching some of his recent interviews he has injected a new term into his spiel: *The Washington Cartel*. Where might that have come from? Two weeks ago six copies of my book Cuba 54 were shipped by Amazon to a Houston Zip Code. In that book I label the Cuban-American politicians who protect murderers and terrorists as the 'Miami Cartel.' Plagiarism?

[167] https://youtu.be/P_BEM64XHXk

Cuban Loquaciousness

There are three men of Cuban heritage who I have studied in depth: Senator Ted Cruz, Pastor Rafael Cruz, and Commandante Fidel Castro. As a retired professional speaker, I have to say that I am impressed by the verbal tenacity of these three Compadres Cubano.

Rafael Cruz can speak before a group for an hour or so without notes, the lines of his act well-rehearsed and committed to memory. Smooth flowing heavily accented words punctuated by flashes of anger are Rafael Cruz's hallmark.

Fidel Castro is a legendary orator, never using notes while giving speeches in Plaza de la Revolucion in Havana for up to five hours. He also holds the record for the longest speech ever at the United Nations.

On September 26, 1960 Fidel Castro made his first appearance at the United Nations as Prime Minister of Cuba. When his time to speak came he opened by saying: "Although it has been said of us that we speak at great length, you may rest assured we will endeavor to be brief." The speech then lasted four and a half hours.

But the most loquacious of these three Cubanos is hands down Senator Ted Cruz. The attorney and former

Solicitor General of Texas has argued before the US Supreme Court nine time. His box score is 5 wins, 4 losses. How ironic since 5-4 is often the Court's final vote on controversial issues. (Rafael Cruz tells audiences that Ted has never lost before SCOTUS; proud Papa's tend to exaggerate)

Before the Supreme Court the speaking time is limited. Where Ted really showed his *machismo Cubano* was on the Senate floor when he led a filibuster seeking to defund Obamacare. The filibuster lasted twenty one hours and nineteen minutes. It started on Tuesday September 24 and ended on Wednesday September 25, 2013 – the day before the 53rd anniversary of Fidel Castro's record-setting speech at the United Nations. Could Ted Cruz have bypassed his Dad Rafael and been channeling Fidel Castro?

Afterthought

Lessons from my Parents

I was so blessed to be raised by two parents, Narcisse & Lillian LeBon who were devout Catholics, deep in their faith, and who always set examples for my siblings and me. My Dad had two cardinal rules: always be a man of your word and never, ever lie. I mention them here because the Cruz men call to mind each of my parents' frequent expressions.

My mother used to say of charlatans like 'pastor' Rafael Cruz who lead amoral and dishonest lives but preach down to everyone around them – *"The biggest sinners pray the loudest,"* their hypocrisy is deafening.

My next oldest brother and I got into a lot of mischief as kids. Whenever we got into a jam and would concoct an alibi together my father would listen to us and then he would say – *"One lies and the other one swears by it."*

This is appropriate for the Cruz men – Rafael concocts the lies and Ted repeats them as gospel truth, and in many cases embellishes them. My father used to admonish my brothers and me: *'If you always tell the truth, the details never change. "* The Cruz men should be so admonished.

Pop had another expression that I have to share and give him props. Whenever he heard someone lying like Rafael Cruz does my father would say, *"If bullshit were concrete that guy could build a super highway."*

Thanks Mom and Dad for raising us to be truthful, and not as Ted Cruz was raised.

Blowback

If conservatives are good at anything, it's playing he role of victim. They get that from the playbook of the accidental governor of Alaska – it's always the media, the libs, etc. out to get her, her twice pregnant out of wedlock daughter, and the rest of her family.

Though his events are generally cloaked in privacy, Rafael Cruz is a public figure. Make no doubt he is out there with his lies and his crazy conspiracy theories and bizarre rhetoric stumping for 'My Ted' to be President of the United States. He claims to have spoken at over 100 pastor's conferences in the past two years.

Some conservatives will attack this book and say that candidates' families are 'off-limits.' They will cite President Obama's statement when he said that back in 2008. They attacked Thomas Roberts of MSNBC who said in March 2015 that he would follow Rafael Cruz with cameras.

Well we are talking apples and oranges. Criticizing two pre-teen girls is reprehensible. Pointing out the lifelong lies, amoral life, and bizarre beliefs of a non-credentialed pastor is fair game. He claims to have been a player in Conservative politics since the Reagan

Campaign of 1980 and is trying to ram his son down the throat of American voters; he is fair game.

To get an even better understanding of Rafael Cruz and why he should come under scrutiny as public orator, read Buzzfeed's collection of *the 68 Most Controversial Things Rafael Cruz Says.*[168]

You can also hear him really unload without all the histrionics on a You Tube recording of a conference call he had with pastors sponsored by a group called STAND – Staying True to America's Natural Destiny.[169]

May God Bless the United States of America, watch over her, and protect her from people like Rafael and Ted Cruz.

---

[168] http://www.buzzfeed.com/ilanbenmeir/the-most-controversial-things-ted-cruzs-dad-has-ever-said#.pkA8JyX1p

[169] https://www.youtube.com/watch?v=LKEt5gfFTUo

Appendix

University of Texas Tuition—www.utwatch.org

ww.utwatch.org/tuition/tuitionstudy.html

Tuition
-Per 15 Hours

	1970	1975	1980	1985	1986	1987
In State Liberal Arts	104	195	226	364	431	435
In State Natural Sciences	104	195	226	364	431	435
Out of State Liberal Arts	254	735	776	1984	1991	1995
Out of State Natural Sciences	254	735	776	1984	1991	1995
Law In State	104	195	226	544	731	915
Law Out of State	254	735	776	2434	2441	2445

My wingman and service dog who gives me
unconditional love, Brady. We were hosted at a reception
in the Cuban Embassy, Washington, DC by
Ambassador José Ramón Cabañas Rodríguez

Photo Gallery on Facebook

https://www.facebook.com/pages/Ted-Cruz-Liar/550231751781834

You Tube Video Channel – All Videos

https://www.youtube.com/channel/UC_E7zWmpN-vOn-U7gAX1_Mg

About the videos of the lies told by Rafael & Ted Cruz: they
are virtually verbatim to the transcribed version in this book.
In some cases there may be some slight variance; this is due
to the fact that while reviewing hours of video in some cases
there were variations of the Cruz lie so what is printed in the
book is a sort of 'hybrid'. In no case were videos mixed
together in order to change the misrepresented message of
the Cruz lie. - PL

Remedial Reading for
Rafael I and Rafael II

The heart is more deceitful than all else – Jeremiah 17:9

Keep your tongue from evil and your lips from speaking deceit. - Psalms 34: 12-13

Therefore, laying aside falsehood, speak truth each one of you with his neighbor for we are members of one another. - Ephesians 4:25

Do not lie to one another, since you laid aside the old self with its evil practices. – Colossians 3:9-10

You shall not steal, nor deal falsely, nor lie to one another. "You shall not swear falsely by My name, so as to profane the name of your God; I am the LORD. – Leviticus 19:11-12

Lying lips are an abomination to the LORD, -Proverbs 12:22

A false witness will not go unpunished, and he who tells lies will perish. – Proverbs 19:9

You destroy those who speak falsehood; The LORD abhors the man of bloodshed and deceit. – Proverbs 5:6

Your tongue devises destruction, Like a sharp razor, O worker of deceit. You love evil more than good, Falsehood more than speaking what is right. Selah. You love all words that devour, O deceitful tongue – Psalms 52: 2-5

"But for the cowardly and unbelieving and abominable and murderers and immoral persons and sorcerers and idolaters and all liars, their part will be in the lake that burns with fire and brimstone, which is the second death.- Revelation 21:8

Made in the USA
Middletown, DE
09 May 2016